Outside Apartment 38

Broken Language Vol. 1

Juni

This book is dedicated to all those people that were on the streets of Washington Heights during the 70s, 80s and 90s, whether they are alive or dead, free or incarcerated. It is also dedicated to all of our kids. I hope that they can learn something from our past and maybe even understand us a little better by getting just a glimpse of what life was like for us in our own youth.

In Loving Memory of Emilia Lopez

Contents

Intro

I don't have that many good memories. The ones that do stand out are small pieces of my childhood, the birth of my kids, meeting my wife, and other little things here and there. Cliché shit. And then I have those things that I like to call happy endings to real bad memories. You know, the type of shit we all go through, such as surviving near-death experiences a couple of times, my mother overcoming illness, and my being released from prison. None of it is really good at all but the final outcome. I guess the bad things we go through have a heavier impact on the mind. At least for me, I know that's the case; it's called trauma. I know it well. I just didn't realize how much I'd come across it in my life until I started writing all the shit I had been through.

For over the past fifteen years, I've occasionally been woken up by nightmares that—no matter where the fuck they start—they always seem to end inside apartment 38, at the address of 600 W. 183rd Street in the Washington Heights neighborhood of New York City. Maybe it's 'cause that apartment once was—and in my subconscious, still is—my safety zone. Home sweet home. A place of family and warmth where I know nobody will ever do me any harm. Or it could just be that within my time of living in that apartment and hanging out in that vicinity even after Moms had moved away, was when I went through the worst of my life; that block and apartment might symbolize my struggles, failures, and fears. It's bugged out 'cause while I was living through it all, I loved every minute of it, everything aside from the deaths of so many of my friends that took place at the time.

Washington Heights took a lot of the people I loved and turned them into murderers, drug addicts, lifelong prisoners, and corpses. I became all of those things too, or as close to them as is possible anyway.

I came up in a hell of a time, a time when murder was the norm. But before my environment turned for the worse, I had a childhood filled with promise. I was just a regular kid like the rest of you once were; a kid who played sports; a little dude with a pencil that liked to draw and write stories; a young teen that fell in love with Hip Hop and turned his pencil lead into poetry and his hands into sharp blades on turntables, his voice into an instrument swerving smoothly on top of a fat-ass track, effortlessly playing alongside drums, basslines, and piano keys.

But somewhere along the birth of crack and the rise of Hip Hop, I lost my way. Hip Hop created an outlet of creativity for me, but crack caused a boom in the coke trade that eventually swept me and my peeps

2

away as if the hood had been hit by a cocaine hurricane that lasted more than a decade.

This is the first book in a series. In this joint (*Broken Language, Volumes 1* and *2*), I mainly look at the first sixteen years of my life to try to see where shit started going wrong for me. I take a couple of glimpses forward into '87 and '88, but it really ends in '86. I started out by writing shit from all over the place, 1970's to 2000's, it was supposed to be a one-off, but for me to fit small pieces of my life into one book and just disregard the rest ain't make sense; I had too much say and accomplish.

As I wrote this one book I was supposed to be writing, my moms asked me why I didn't write of more positive experiences; I told her I couldn't remember too many. I mean, the insanity we were living in was fun to me at the time, but now I see just how bad it really was; there was nothing positive about it at all. Who knows, maybe the bad just outweighs the good. Or maybe I just have to work through the bad first so that the good could just peek out a little every now and then. Maybe I'll be able to write about the good times later in life after I get all the bad off my chest.

This shit is therapy.

After episodes of writing brought pain and feelings of being looked at differently by certain friends and family, I would stop and find it hard to continue for months at a time. I knew I had to speak to my mother for guidance. She knew a lot about of my life on the street, but for years I kept her in the dark about the more heinous things me and my friends

3

were involved in. When I finally decided to open up and tell her what was holding me back from finishing—the wild shit she ain't know about—she cringed as she smoked her stogie, and was stunned at first, like any good parent should be. But Moms still gave me her blessings. She told me to just write from the heart, that my life was my life and it was better to tell my life than to tell a lie.

"God gave you that skill so you can tell your story. After all you have been through, he has you here for a reason. Don't let anyone hold you back from your dreams, baby." *Mami* said.

I took her advice.

As time passed, I sometimes told her of incidents that had happened in detail. Moms would make a screw-face or open her eyes in horror as she took pulls off one Parliament after another.

"Do you have to put that in your book?" she asked one time.

I wondered if she was having second thoughts.

"A true story is not so true if the harsh realities of life are left out, Moms. That type of realness is what makes it good."

"Yeah…you're right."

Moms then sat up straight in her chair and made a proud face like we were about to do something big.

"Do your thing, baby."

After nearly seven years of writing random incidents that spanned over three decades, I started filling in the gaps and stitching everything together. When I learned to format my pages, I was thrown for a loop when I realized what I had planned on being just one book had ballooned up to enough material for a book series. I had created a monster. You know how it goes: a beautiful monster, the kind that's ugly but you just can't stop looking at. Or, at least that's what I hope for.

When writing memoirs, most writers from the inner-city streets put their whole lives inside of one book and at the end it's almost always a happy ending; they wind up some sort of college-educated professionals, or executives even. Not the case with me. I have no formal training in writing aside from elementary and junior high. Yeah, I went to high school, but I never really went to high school; it was a hangout (I did ninth grade like three times, I think). Most of my skill comes from over thirty years of writing rhymes, reading books and devouring newspapers front to back. On the work front, I've mostly held one dead-end job after another. I'm not college-educated and I'm only an executive of what's in front of you right now. This is it for me. I'm gonna drop a couple of these books and see where my writing takes me. And even if it doesn't do anything spectacular for me, I'll still continue writing, 'cause just like Sadat X said, *I'm still nice with the verbs, so fuck what'chu heard.*

So, yo, enough with the bullshit. Sit the fuck back, light up a blunt, or do whatever it is you do, throw on a couple of dope-ass instrumentals produced by the likes of Pete Rock, DJ Premier, and Havoc—don't forget Marley Marl, RZA, Large Professor, The Beatminerz, D.I.T.C. and L.E.S.—and let me proceed to take you on a journey through my bugged out walk of life.

Graffiti-stained subway trains

entertained my young brain

way before the drugs came

& witnessing guns' flames

walls bombed like napalm

by Lee, Dondi, & the one Sane

as I rode from Times Square

thoughts flowed & I made my first rhymes there

looking at the pieces

characters ranged from the devil to Jesus

homeless people on the train had it smellin' like feces

Fearless Four played when a goon popped

a tape in a boombox

as he leaned on the doors

in a BVD, shorts, Pumas, & tube socks

there were men in business suits

I had my Buster Brown boots

before I wore Timbs,

the Deuce was loose with prostitutes

triple feature at the theatre

the audience was a freak show

Diesel, Dust & Weed

pumped right in front of the peep shows

my mind was filled with rhymes

& small petty crimes

living thru hard times

while riding the 1 line

hanging out with Ant & Juni

life got more gloomy

when Crack hit the hood

me & my boys got loony

there was no more bombin'

seeing dead bodies was common

I advanced in my rhymin'

but losing my life was just a matter of timin'

kids with who I played Hide & Seek

committed suicide & homicide on the streets

I wish I could just go back to the train ride & the beats...

RIP

Ant & Juni

"...Cop a bottle of crack/ five minutes flat/ they back"

Night of the Living Baseheads

A school night, 1985. Highbridge Park.

"Okay, listen! This is the only way I'm gonna hook you up!" yelled
a slim, dark-skinned teenager whose tag was Skemo.

"Talk to me, Skemo!" said the male crackhead.

"Dime, negrito!" repeated the female one.

The other female fiend—the pretty one—intently stared at Skemo,
quietly waiting for his proposal.

Skemo was standing in the darkness of the park backed by a quartet
of trees—his chest pumped out—feeling like a general among his peers,
a bunch of other young teens. In reality, he was just a pitcher working
for somebody else. But since he was the only one out there handling
money and crack bottles, he was feeling like a big shot; selling drugs

was something for him and every other lost kid in my hood to feel proud of at the time.

After twenty minutes of them hassling, pleading, and trying to run game on him for some crack on credit, he loved how easy it was to get all three of them to quiet down and submit to him. The power he had over these broken human beings was as addictive as the crack they were begging him for.

"Go in the sandlot!"

Muñeco and Reyna glanced over at the sandlot for a fraction of a second. Patty didn't take her eyes off of Skemo, their daily puppet master until the shift change at midnight; that's when Spanky usually took over.

"All three of you, take off your clothes! Reyna, you lay on your back! Patty, you take that bottle and put it in Reyna's pussy!" said Skemo, motioning to an empty Heineken bottle that had been discarded on the ground. "You have to fuck her with it! And while they doing that...Muñeco, you gonna fuck Patty... doggystyle!"

Some kids' jaws dropped, others began laughing hysterically and screaming shit like, "Oh, you fuckin' crazy, Skemo!" and "Coño, I can't wait to see this shit!" I was in between that, on oh shit mode, my mind blown away after the preview of what Skemo had just said flashed through my head.

"How much you gonna give us?!" asked Reyna.

"One! For all three of you could share it!"

"Let's gooooo!" Muñeco almost sounded like he was harmonizing as he became animated, taking his shirt off mad fast while rushing towards the sandlot.

"Nah, man! No way! Vete pal carajo! (Go to hell!) I ain't doing that shit for only one rock!" yelled Reyna.

"Then get the fuck outta here and stop begging me, bitch! I could find another crackhead that will do it!" Skemo yelled back.

Patty was still staring at him. Still dressed in clean clothes, she was the only one of the three who you could tell was still bathing regularly and hadn't yet fallen all the way down into the crack hole. The skin on her beautiful cream-colored face looked as smooth and soft as a model's and her 5'2 physique was still thick enough to get her asked out on a date. Patty was stupid fine.

Reyna, on the other hand, her dark beauty was damaged. It resembled a rough terrain of skid marks, potholes, and train tracks. She still had meat on her, but it was an old saggy thickness.

Muñeco was a few shades between them, more brown than white. He also had things on his face he hadn't been born with. The way his body looked—a worn out frame of skin on bones—let me know he hadn't eaten anything but crack pipes for a while.

"C'mon, man, at least give us one rock each! Muñeco be hogging that shit up every time!" Reyna pleaded. That's when I knew Skemo had made them do some other crazy shit before.

"Nah, fuck that!" Skemo replied. "That's your problem, not mine! Any second now another bitch is gonna come in the park and she'll take that bottle in her ass with a smile on her face, while you only gonna get to watch, so go get your popcorn!"

"C'mon, girls, let's get this going!" yelled Muñeco from the sandlot. "I wanna smoke already!"

"Skemo, c'mon, man! Just give me two for me alone and I swear I'll let her stick that bottle in me! And then I'll suck your dick, too, man! Stop being stingy!" Reyna's words were real fast and stuck together like one long word instead of thirty-two. She was begging now. Her mannerisms were anxious and manic.

"Ah-ight, bussit! I'll hook you up with two bottles! Two bottles for all three of you, take it or leave it!"

Patty immediately turned around, walked to the sandlot, and began undressing. We were all stuck on her flawless body.

"Goddamn stingy motherfucker, this is the last time...." Reyna mumbled as she hesitantly followed Patty.

"Last time, last time, that's what the fuck you said last time! Just shut the fuck up and get busy, bitch, before I smack the shit outta you! You gotta earn yours, baby!" Skemo shouted.

"Nah, you ain't right, Skemo."

"C'mon, Reyna, you know I got love for you! If I didn't, I wouldn't even be hooking you up!"

That incident could have ended a lot worse.

Throughout the stretch of 1985 to 1995, Hip Hop's golden era and the crack era—the worst time in my city—I had seen crackheads beaten within an inch of their lives too many times. Being raped, tortured and

13

murdered was an everyday thing, too; the only thing that kept them alive was their addiction, that craving to smoke another rock. But Reyna was lucky that night.

The fact that Skemo knew these people by their real names made me wonder about if he had known them before the crack wave; had they been neighbors of his, people who saw him grow up, maybe even looked out for him in the past, occasionally hooked him up with some change for candy and ice cream like so many of the older peeps from the hood did with the younger ones. At worst, at least one of them could have even been a relative of his. It wasn't a longshot; selling crack to your own brother, sister, father, and mother wasn't unheard of. Or maybe they were just your typical crackheads, who bought but mostly begged from Skemo; who hung around him so much because he had the magic rock, that for him working the night shift in the park had become like living in a twisted community where he had no choice but to eventually learn all its residents' names.

Regardless, the whole scene was crazy. I was only fifteen years old, watching a demented threesome with a dirty bottle take place in the sandlot where so many innocent kids played at daily. Nighttime at the park was already as dark as fuck but what was happening in front of my eyes and all around me had cast a feeling of an even more profound darkness, something evil. In time, many including myself would become a part of that evil as it transformed itself into normalcy and an everyday way of life.

It wasn't quite there yet, but crack would eventually devastate my hood to a point beyond which any amount of words could ever explain. "Hell on earth" is probably the best I can do, and that episode at the park was only the beginning.

Going Way Back

My name on the streets used to be Static. Even though I never took my graffiti habit past pieces of loose-leaf paper, my boy Kid Tase suggested it when I was in need of a tag name. He felt it suited me; to him I was an alleged troublemaker. But nah, I was just a feisty little dude. Kid Tase misconstrued debating for troublemaking; we always argued. The thing was, if you tried to hit me over the head with some bullshit, I would tell you to your face that you were lying; I would come at you from mad different angles without letting up just to prove you were a liar. When lying to me, my boys needed to be prepared for a day in court, 'cause my cross-examination was definitely coming strong if shit ain't sound right. Blowing holes in their bullshit was too easy.

I didn't really like the sound of "Static", but I still ran with it just so I wouldn't be the only one in the crew being called by his government name; "Gustavo" and "Gus" just didn't mesh well with Kid Tase, Disco, Moe, Little Jay, R-Daddy and Poppa Pete.

When I got into my late twenties, the younger cats on the block started calling me Stat Da Don because of all the shit I had been through and survived, shit I had incorporated into the rhymes I spit for them on a daily basis; I was the only one from our crew that had been able to slip through the system and dodge convictions multiple times; I got away from the cops all the time, and the times they did arrest me, nine times out of ten it was for some simple shit like smoking weed or hopping the train, nothing serious. When it *was* serious, it was *real* serious, A-1 type-shit. But I still beat those too. So, because of all that bullshit and more, my little homies considered me an OG—Stat Da Don. It was cool to have as a rap name, but on the real, I was just me, a regular cat just like them that was out there doing and witnessing a lot of crazy shit; a kid with a story to tell, not some gangsta-monster-serial killer dude, especially not at 120 lbs.

Now, I hate to start this off by telling you my date of birth like everybody else does it, but fuck it, you might need to know that shit later on anyway, so let's set this shit off already.

I was born on September 9th, 1970.

It was also my *abuelo's* birthday, my father's father, that being the reason why I was given the name Gustavo, same as him. But that wasn't the only coincidence on that date, because on that night in 1961—two years after Fidel Castro took over Cuba—my father and nineteen others escaped that country on a big-ass motorboat. Castro's coast guard chased them over a long stretch of the Atlantic Ocean and initiated a violent shootout when they realized my father and his boys were getting closer to the Bahamas. None of my father's crew got hit.

Earlier that day, my father and a ragtag crew of some of his closest friends—and other cats he didn't even know—met up at my grandparents' house with all the guns and bullets they could get their hands on. My father was the youngest. Him and his homies weren't fuckin' around; their mindset was a combination of a few of the best Hip Hop album titles to ever come out, 'cause they were set on getting the fuck out of Cuba By Any Means Necessary, and Ready to Die Trying if it had to be that way.

For two of them, both were accomplished.

But first, their boat's motor died, and they drifted for five days without any food and water until being found and towed to Nassau. All their guns—except one that was stashed in a cooler—were confiscated on the spot by the local authorities, and they were given the option of leaving the island on their own within twenty-four hours or getting sent back to Cuba in shackles.

They chose to keep it moving.

As they resumed their trek to Miami the next morning, the boat's engine gave out again in the middle of the sea. After a few more days lost, they had all become distraught and hopeless; the combination of starvation, thirst, heat exhaustion, and seeing nothing but endless waters and skies for days on end took its toll on them. Two men committed suicide by self-inflicted gunshots. Their bodies were thrown into the sea.

Altogether, it took fourteen days for my father and the other defectors to reach Miami.

I can't tell you how much of this is true 'cause my father's memory ain't what it used to be. Nowadays, he even claims that singer, actor, and activist Harry Belafonte was in Nassau to perform the day the refugees arrived and had arranged for them to stay at the same hotel as him, feeding them and having them attend one of his shows. But what definitely did happen was the escape, the stop in the Bahamas, and the days lost at sea.

Every time he told his story, my father would end it off by saying, *"I was pissed off when they took them because I really liked one of those guns, a real shiny one we had."*

Guns…

Bullets…

I had heard this story of my father's great escape mad times, but I had never thought guns and bullets would make their way into my life someday, not with the way we were living; to me it seemed we pretty much had everything we wanted as kids; bad guys with guns and shootouts in the streets only existed on TV shows, you know, *Baretta* and *Kojak* type of shit. That hard life of poverty and grittiness just couldn't be real. Shit, after leaving the streets of New York City in the early seventies, the areas that served as our neighborhoods consisted of the beautiful homes and clean, peaceful streets of towns in Connecticut and Puerto Rico.

That is, until we moved back to New York.

My birthplace is Washington Heights, the best hood on this planet. Nowadays it's considered Little Dominican Republic. But back then it was a predominantly Greek, Irish, and Jewish neighborhood in upper Manhattan, right above Harlem. Puerto Ricans and Cubans made up the majority of the Latinos living there at the time, while Dominican, Ecuadorian, and African-American families were only in small pockets. We even had a few Chinese peeps up there, including some of the Chinese Cubans, who had first settled or been born in Cuba before coming to NYC and opening numerous restaurants. They spoke Spanish fluently.

The notorious South Bronx was right across the bridge from us, but Washington Heights had the appearance of a newly-built city compared to the burnt down buildings and decay of the Boogie Down. It was a real safe place to live back in those days, nearly the equivalent of the upscale neighborhoods of midtown Manhattan. We lived on 178th Street, between the avenues of Broadway and Wadsworth.

My earliest and only memory of that apartment is of my father and me in a dark room one night, watching a Mohammed Ali boxing match on a small black-and-white TV, and my father constantly trying to fix the picture by adjusting the wire hanger he used as an antenna. It plays over and over in my head, the image of Ali gliding in the boxing ring on that grainy television screen, my agitated father continuously getting up from the bed, messing with his homemade antenna. I was mesmerized.

To this day, it's the only sport I follow. Boxing is the only thing my father ever taught me to love. He never really took the time to try and teach me how to love the more important things in life, such as family, work, education, or even myself. What I may have picked up from him but ain't notice until much later was his hustling skills and a little bit of his running from responsibilities, not to mention his willpower to escape tough situations.

The art of escaping must run in my family.

At the age of one, two babysitters we had never seen before took my three-year-old sister Cookie and me to Central Park for a picnic. After taking pictures of us, they laid down on a blanket spread over the grass and closed their eyes. I don't know what went through Cookie's head at that moment, but she must have figured since they were napping, it was time for us to get the fuck out of there and get back to our family; she grabbed my stroller and made a run for it. Cookie's steering was good—and according to what the babysitters later told our mother, she had an ecstatic smile on her face as she ran through the field—until the ground beneath us got too bumpy; that's when Cookie lost control of my stroller and it turned over on its side with me inside of it. I didn't get hurt *that* time, but it was the first of too many accidents I would go on to have involving moving vehicles, and the last getaway plan Cookie would put me down with.

After I turned two years old, my family moved to Bridgeport. My uncle Raul and a few of his and my father's acquaintances from their childhood days in Cuba—plus one of my mother's younger sisters, *Titi*

Sylvia—had all bounced from New York City for the slower-paced towns of Connecticut, and Moms decided we should follow. My father stayed behind, running his candy store for a few more months and only coming through on weekends before finally staying with us for good.

The first house my parents rented was on Center Street. The only thing I remember about it is the front yard. I guess the reason for that is because of what happened there a few months after we moved in: I almost got murdered.

Three Feet High & Rising

My first brush with death was at three years old.

We had an Italian family living next-door to us at the time, and according to my parents, a lot of the Italians in the area didn't like the flood of Latino families migrating into the neighborhood.

Our co-existence with that family was peppered with dirty looks and negative comments they tried to conceal in their lingo. But their facial expressions and words in Italian that were similar to Spanish gave it all away. When they did exchange greetings with my parents, their "hellos" were more like "I don't wanna be bothered". My parents did their best to ignore it.

I wonder how they would have felt if they had known my pop's mother was actually born to Italian parents in Brooklyn before they relocated to Cuba when she was still a little girl.

My sisters and I were too young to know of or recognize any type of prejudice, and I don't know if the children of that household were exposed to the hate their parents had for us, but we all played together anyway. The kids who lived there were two little girls and their younger brother. He was about five.

So, one day while we were all playing outside on our front lawn, the boy slung a rope around my neck. I thought we were about to play some new shit.

What game is this?

He then crossed the rope over itself, pulled back his arms and squeezed it with all he had as if he were tying a fuckin' knot on his sneakers. Our sisters were off to the side playing their own game, so they ain't immediately notice this little motherfucker killing me. I felt the rope tighten and my eyes tear up as my tiny fingers tried to loosen its grasp, but he just maintained his grip and squeezed even tighter. My eyes felt like they were gonna burst out of their sockets. I got light-headed and kinda dizzy and probably was about to fall out when my sister Aggie saw what was going on, pushed the kid to the ground, and took the rope off of me.

As I wheezed for some air in my lungs, my sisters went on and on about how I was almost purple in the face, but all I could think of was how the other kid's face was a picture of absolute anger, blood-red as he choked the shit out of me.

These days, I wonder if he was even playing at all, or was he acting out something he might've overheard his father say he would like to do to all the nasty Cubans and Puerto Ricans moving into the hood. Fuck 'em.

Less than a year later, we moved again, this time into a three-story home on William Street, a few blocks from my uncle's crib. This house was huge. It had a backyard, a basement, and an attic. The first floor had an enormous living room, the kitchen, and a dining area. Upstairs there were three bedrooms and a bathroom.

My family used to say that house was haunted because every night you could hear the steps creaking as if someone was walking up the stairs. My sisters and I used to count the footsteps, fifteen to the second floor and eleven to the attic. It ain't help that my father liked to frighten us with his pranks. He'd do things like lie down flat on the hallway floor, covered completely in a white blanket, and then wait until we came out of the bedroom, so he could jump up and scare the shit out of us.

The homeowners, Virginia and her mother Stella, lived on the other side of the staircase wall; it was a two-family home divided down the middle. They were quiet old ladies who kept to themselves; I don't remember them ever saying a word to me. But as a child, there were a few things that made them a little creepy: they looked exactly alike; same hairdo, same glasses, even same outfit, except Stella was at least a foot taller than Virginia. If Virginia was in her seventies, then Stella had to have been almost a hundred. Every day they wore the same black and white dresses that reminded me of the pilgrims I was being taught about in my kindergarten class. Their family had built that house in the early 1900's. When Stella died in late '74, that's when we supposedly noticed there was a ghost walking up the stairs of our home.

On Saturdays, Moms used to run our family's bodega for a few hours while my father went in his wood-paneled station wagon to get more shit from the wholesalers. By then, my oldest sister Aggie was thirteen, old enough to take care of us. My uncle's three daughters occasionally came through and all seven of us played for hours throughout that big house.

Kids being kids, sometimes games turned cruel.

One time we were coming down from the attic. My sister Leticia and one of my twin cousins were leading the way out when they tried to shut the door behind them and lock the two smallest kids—Cookie and me—inside. We weren't having it. Cookie and I used all the strength we had in our little bodies to give those pre-teens a fuckin' challenge. That door was an inch from being closed shut all the way, and our feet kept sliding backwards, but after Cookie and I momentarily looked at a door behind us that led to Virginia's side of the house, we panicked and pushed and pushed until they gave up and let us out. I came out of there exhausted and out of breath, but it felt good to win.

That victory wouldn't last long.

It might not have been on that same day, but one time I was shoved into the basement and locked in. Cookie wasn't there to help me that time. I banged on the door and cried for my sisters and cousins to let me out, but they just laughed on the other side. It soon seemed like they forgot about me and continued playing throughout other parts of the house, 'cause after a couple of short minutes, I ain't even hear them no more.

When I got tired of screaming and banging, I turned and sat at the top of the old wooden staircase and quietly cried. After a few more minutes, I calmed down and started analyzing my surroundings while my hands took turns wiping my wet face. The basement was almost a complete blackness. It was dusty and full of cobwebs. A washing machine, clotheslines, and a bunch of junk was partially visible 'cause of a dim light that shined from a corner of the room. When I lowered my head to see where the light was coming from, it was a small lamp. What I saw next caught me off guard: the lamp made a perfectly round spotlight over a mannequin head that was on a table underneath it. Seeing that was all it took for me to jump up and hysterically yell and bang on that door again until my hands were sore. The thoughts of my dad's scary pranks, coupled with the belief of ghosts on the stairs, and now this chopped-off head in my basement, caused me to scream myself hoarse. I was fucked up.

I don't know how long I lasted in there, but as a little four-year-old kid, it felt like a long-ass time. As a matter of fact, I don't even remember when I was let out. A piece of me might still be in that fuckin' basement.

Either I got over my fear of the mannequin head real fast or went totally insane, 'cause that summer, while watching the movie *Jaws* in a packed movie theatre, when a scene came on where a severed head or some shit like that was shown floating underwater, I busted out laughing

27

while everybody else was stunned. I must have been thinking some shit like *"that's nothing, I got a real head in my basement."* My sister Aggie looked at me as if I was disturbed. She's always said she knew something wasn't right about me ever since then.

Man, as for that ghost bullshit, I'm sure that was Virginia walking up the stairs of her own house the whole time. I mean, she did live on the other side of the wall; *her stairs* were beside *our stairs*. We probably never heard her in the daytime 'cause of all the damn noise we made ourselves.

There was this crazy little white boy named Leroy that lived in the house next to ours. Every now and then he would burst out of his house butt-naked and make a run for it like an escaped convict. His obese mom would chase out after him and snatch him up in a bear hug outside their picket fence while Leroy kicked his feet and swung his arms, trying to get loose from her with his little nuggets jiggling all around. Leroy might have been wild, but at least he was funny and wasn't trying to kill me like the little demon kid on Center Street.

My family's routine on most school mornings went like this: Pops headed out to go open his grocery store at 7 AM, we all got dressed and had breakfast, and then me and Moms walked Cookie and Leticia to school before meeting up with Pops to work with him; Aggie rode a bus to Junior High School. Twice a week, my father dropped Moms and me off early to open the store so that he could go pick up more merchandise from the wholesalers. That's when Cookie and Leticia—who were only six and nine-years-old at the time—were left alone at the house with Leticia having the responsibility of getting them to school.

I know. It was a dangerous decision on my parents' part, but they only did it so that they wouldn't lose any business at the bodega. I don't think they were being neglectful, but naïve, thinking things in the U.S. of A. were the same as in their own countries, where kids were left unsupervised all the time without any repercussions. Plus, whereas today it's splashed all over TV screens all the time, people back then weren't exposed to the horrors of predators like pedophiles and kidnappers at all. I'm sure the tranquility of the town of Bridgeport must have also clouded their judgment at the time. I can't blame them, though, that shit did seem like *The Brady Bunch* neighborhood with its picket fences and tree-lined streets and blonde families.

But one time, two raggedy-looking Black men did show up at the back door we had in the kitchen and tried to let themselves in after noticing my sisters and me were alone; they fidgeted with the doorknob and pushed a few times while staring at us through the little square windows on the door. But the locks didn't budge, so they finally gave up and bounced.

Anyway, one morning when they were running late for class, Leticia stopped Cookie as they were approaching their school. She nervously explained how by being late they would now have to go in through the main entrance, which meant having to walk by the dreaded principal's office. I guess to Cookie that sounded like they had to pass by the big bad wolf's house.

"What are we going to do?" asked Cookie.

"Maybe we should go back home."

Cookie rolled with it. Fortunately for Leticia, Cookie was mad young at the time and still hadn't acquired the by-the-book attitude she has today; Cookie don't play; she has never broke laws and does not bend rules.

Back at the house, my sisters decided they would keep their school-cutting adventure a secret. They cleaned up the house real quick, just like they would have done after school, and then went upstairs to play with their dolls.

After a while had passed, they were startled by the sound of someone opening the front door on the first floor. They ran from one bedroom to the next to try to hide.

"Hide in the closet! I'll hide under the bed!"

Cookie initially did as she was told, but just after a few seconds, she freaked out and slid under the bed with Leticia.

They heard more than one pair of footsteps rush up the stairs and into my parents' bedroom. The heavy footsteps then slowly walked into their hiding area. A hand reached under the foot of the bed and began to lift it up off the floor. The first thing Cookie and Leticia saw then was a big black revolver pointing at them. They thought their lives were over. As the bed was lifted even higher and the intruders revealed themselves, my sisters then saw who it was holding the burner in his hand.

"*Papi*, don't shoot!" Please don't kill us, daddy!" my sisters screamed while immediately breaking into tears.

"Coño! Qué carajo hacen ustedes aquí?!" ("Fuck! What the hell are you doing here?!"), my father furiously shouted back. He and a friend had stopped by the house to pick something up.

"We're sorry, daddy! Don't kill us!" they repeatedly begged.

It wasn't the first time Leticia had seen my father's gun; a couple of months before, he had pointed it at my mother's face and pulled the trigger. Lucky for Moms, the barrel was empty. Whether my father knew that and just meant to scare my mother, or he forgot to load bullets into it, we'll never find out.

After going off on my sisters, my father made them kneel on the floor and face the wall in separate corners of the room. He ordered them to stay there and not move until he got back to the house. After about an hour of kneeling and quietly staring at the wall, the phone rang. Leticia immediately got up to answer it.

"Hello?" she greeted, in her innocent and curious voice.

"Yo no le dije a ustedes que no se muevan?!" ("Didn't I tell you not to move?!"), my father yelled on the other end of the line.

Leticia hung up the phone and ran back to her punishment spot. Always one to take chances, she got up one more time to turn on the TV. She and Cookie sat on their butts and watched *All My Children* and *One Life to Live* from those corners until Moms got to the crib to bail them out.

Sure, we laugh at this story when it's brought up at family gatherings, but as thoughtless and brutal as my father could be at times, my sisters were extremely lucky that he didn't shoot through that bed without looking first.

Killing one another on some savage shit
for the status of glamorous
cocaine got the hood on smash, guns blast
for a few grams of it

Self-Destruction

Summer 1987. My block. 5 P.M.

A tall man in shorts and a t-shirt runs into my block. An army of angry faces of multiple shades is chasing him and cuts him off right at the corner of John's Fried Chicken. He's Latino, which is rare. The ones being chased are usually Black men—one, a duo, or a pack of three, never more than that. They are usually drug dealers from New Jersey that came to cop some weight, and figured it didn't look hard to rob their favorite coke spot, or stick-up kids posing as drug dealers that came to cop some weight, tied up workers and maybe even bosses, and stole anything from a couple of ounces up to a few kilos, and all the guns and cash too.

But this one is Dominican.

They're beating him with their fists, feet, sticks, bottles, and anything else they can pick up. I recognize most of them, fellas that work in spots throughout the next three blocks up.

The battered man kinda looks like he could be a crackhead. I can't really tell; his appearance changed fast after they caught him, meaning I remember him more as the mask of blood that he's become within a minute or two on my block and not who he was beforehand. Maybe he stole a bundle of crack stashed under a tire or by the garbage bags out on one of the blocks or climbed through the window of a spot and took all the coke.

Horrified bystanders and customers inside John's Fried Chicken—that stop chewing the hairy-looking chicken—stare in shock as he's destroyed right outside the chicken spot's window. He's on his knees with his hands out at his sides as if he's begging for mercy, asking for forgiveness, when another bottle crashes on his blood-soaked, sad clown face. He drops.

It's the first time I see this happen but far from the last. After this, most of them will be Black men. Most times, they'll be running for dear life, and it'll be one of us that'll stop them on our block, usually with a thrown milk crate that trips them up, before the avalanche of fists, feet, bottles and anything else rains on them—one, a duo, or a pack of three, never more than that.

Me and the fellas from my block get involved for the sake of our community—for the love of our hometown drug dealers and killers that are now becoming so common—so that our hood will be respected. Rob one of us and you have to rob all of us.

All the schemers that wanna try robbing a drug spot, thinking it looks easy to pull it off, have no idea that they'll have to fight my whole neighborhood in order to make a clean getaway. A lot of bloody beatdowns will go down at this intersection.

Puerto Rico

In what had to be a combination of my mother missing her homeland, and my father cooking up some magnificent scheme of how he could make crazy money, my family then moved to Levittown, a neighborhood in Toa Baja, Puerto Rico.

Living in Puerto Rico was kind of like living inside of a sunny oven; it was scorching hot around the clock. Every time I stepped outside, it felt like my skin was gonna peel right off as soon as the sunrays touched it. But I loved it, though.

We lived on a dead-end street that led into a grassy trail with a creek, our shortcut to school. At night, it was a mad dark block, and the backdrop of that dead-end only amplified that. But what I remember most about it is that my sisters and I were allowed to play outside a lot more often than in Connecticut; we were out on the block running free instead of just in a fenced backyard. Plenty of other kids lived there, so every evening after dinner our street got packed like a recreation center.

La Séptima (The Seventh) was an eventful block.

Our dog Pimp followed Aggie to her high school by the beach one morning and got run over on an intersection. That was only a few weeks after I messed with him and tried to psyche him out by jumping up on the *marquesina* gate. He jumped up behind me and ripped the ass off my shorts—exposing my tighty-whiteys to the entire block. On that day, I probably learned that besides just barking and running fast, dogs could jump pretty high too. And yeah, his name really was Pimp.

One night while playing out front, the loose basketball hoop on our driveway finally fell off and grazed Cookie's forehead. She brought her hand up to where she felt a slight burn and the tip of her index finger disappeared into her dome-piece. Seconds later, her face was covered in blood. I remember Cookie standing frozen on the spot, panicking and screaming like crazy, looking like that skinny little white girl in *Carrie*.

The three sisters that lived next-door to us had nests of *piojos* in their scalps. That's lice, homie; little nasty bugs that stick to your head like leeches while sucking on you like a two-dollar hoe.

Whenever all the kids stood around talking kid shit, the sisters engaged in convo, too, but all three were scratching their heads intensely with anxious expressions on their grills. Even when running, those bitches had at least one arm up with their hands digging deep into their long, puffy batches of black hair over crazed faces.

38

Their home was filthy; the carpets were basically massive sponges of dog urine. But the parents still allowed their baby boy to crawl on them butt-ass naked.

The day Moms found two *piojos* in Cookie's head, Cookie turned that into breaking news; gossip of *The Three Sisters with Piojos On the Block* was running rampant for a while amongst kids *and* parents. A few kids were quarantined for up to a month.

Another time, a kid threw a cinderblock down at me from the roof of his house and caught the ass whipping of a lifetime; his parents took turns letting loose their belts on him like it was a tag team match. But unlike the Italian kid in Connecticut, there definitely wasn't any racism involved in that attack; it was just another Puerto Rican kid like me having fun, trying to crush his friend similar to the kinda shit we were watching daily on the *Woody Woodpecker* and *Bugs Bunny* cartoons.

One late afternoon, my father was getting ready to go pick up my sisters from school. I wanted to come along but he ain't wanna take me. I went outside and looked around and our block was deserted; none of the other kids were outside. I had to have been bored outta my mind 'cause I was determined to go on that little ride with my father no matter what.

My pops had this thing he always did throughout his life where he would make a few false head starts out the door. He'd walk out to leave, and then go back inside to get his keys, come back out and turn around again to retrieve his wallet; walk out another time, and then realize he had to use the bathroom. It was always the same routine before he finally did leave the house.

Well, on that day, while he was going back and forth, I had decided it would be a good idea to hide in the backseat of his car and surprise him when we got to my sisters' school. After he went back in the house for a second time, I climbed into his car and crouched down behind the passenger seat. I pulled the car door gently behind me so that he wouldn't hear it slamming shut. That could've been a fatal mistake, though; since I didn't pull it hard enough, the door only *appeared* to be closed.

My pops then jumped in his ride and sped off in a hurry. He must have been doing about forty miles per hour. As he reached the end of the block, he busted a sharp left turn which made my little five-year-old, forty-pound body go off-balance and tumble against—and through— the unlocked door. Yeah, that's right; I fell out of the car, flying headfirst onto the concrete.

I rolled a few times and came to a stop at the feet of a lady who was sweeping the front of her driveway. When I think of it now, it makes me laugh; I was on my back, dazed and confused like I'd just had my first weed blunt, not knowing how the fuck I got there, looking at this lady— in a bathrobe and with rollers in her hair—screaming at the top of her lungs.

Meanwhile, my father kept racing down the street until he suddenly came to a screeching halt at that next corner. He must've heard that lady screaming and caught sight of her standing over me in his rearview mirror.

"*Ghos*?!" Pops yelled, tearing my nickname apart with his thick accent. "*Ghos*?!" he yelled again, as if he wasn't sure if that was me. I don't know, maybe he was expecting me to raise my hand as if I was in class while I lay there fucked up on my back.

My father then drove the car in reverse just as fast as he did going forward and stopped right next to where I lay. Lucky me, he didn't run me over. Pops looked worried sick as his eyes concentrated on my forehead.

"*Hijo, que hiciste*?" ("Son, what did you do?")

He then picked me up, laid me down on the backseat, and kept it moving like a racecar driver. I didn't experience any pain on my body, but I felt too tired to move. It could have been that I was going through shock, or maybe the brunt of the fall just rendered me into exhaustion. We picked up my sisters, dropped them off at home, and then my parents and I were off to the nearest Emergency Room.

At the hospital, people kept glancing over at me, particularly at my forehead. My father and mother took turns carrying me. They kept telling me to not fall asleep.

"*Cuando los niños se dan en la cabeza, si se duermen, mas nunca se despiertan*." ("When little kids hit their heads, if they fall asleep, they never wake up again."), my father cautioned me.

He scared the shit out of me when he said that. But more importantly, I had never heard the sound of fear in my father's voice

41

before. Both my parents had a look on their faces I had never seen or noticed before; they were more scared than I was.

"*Yo quiero ver la corta'.*" ("I wanna see the cut.").

My father borrowed my mother's make-up kit from her purse and brought its mirror up to my face. I had a bump the size of a golf ball on the middle of my forehead. It was laced with an inch-long slit in the center of it, making me look like I was growing another fuckin' eye. It was a weird cut; it wasn't bleeding but I could see dark red flesh on the inside.

After three long-ass hours, a doctor still hadn't seen me. Pops complained to the nurses on duty, but he'd soon find out that on that night it would be common for a five-year-old with a head injury to not receive medical attention in a hurry.

My parents got restless and took me to another hospital, but the same thing happened. Another couple of hours passed and I was struggling to stay awake. Pops kept patting me on the cheeks to keep me up.

"*No te duermas, papi, no te duermas.*" ("Don't fall asleep."), my father quietly pleaded.

Understaffing had us so fucked up that I wasn't treated until we got to a third hospital. My parents were freaked out that I might've had internal bleeding of the brain since there wasn't any blood leaking out of the cut, but thanks to the big man upstairs, it was nothing serious; not even stitches were needed.

We got back home at five in the morning, and just a few hours later, I was back outside, running around on our dead–end street again, this time with a gauze on my forehead, happy to have skipped school and have the whole block to myself.

Potholes In My Lawn

At the end of my first-grade schoolyear, we moved to my grandma's block. It was in a better-looking neighborhood than the previous one. The pavement on the sidewalks and streets ain't have no cracks in it, the lawns were well maintained, and the homes were more modern, which made it seem like we were in a wealthier part of town. Shit, even the palm trees looked healthier and brand new out the box with shiny leaves on them. Instead of an ugly dead-end street, this time my parents rented a house at the end of a beautiful cul-de-sac. Grandma lived in the house in front of ours while my aunt, *Titi Paquita*, and her husband Rafael, owned a home only a couple of doors down from her.

Grandma spent most of her time in the *marquesina*, which is basically an open-air garage most of the homes in Puerto Rico have. Instead of garage doors, *marquesinas* have floor-to-ceiling-sized gates at the front to keep out intruders, and most are used as outdoor living rooms. Grandma used to watch her favorite shows on a small color television as she rocked back and forth on her rocking chair. She would prepare a meal by twelve o'clock, have lunch, and afterwards disappear into the house for her *siesta*.

By mid-afternoon, Grandma was back in her rocking chair. Kids would run up to the gate requesting different flavors of the *limber* (Puerto Rican ice) she sold for ten cents apiece.

"*Doña Paca! Doña Paca! Me puede dar uno de limón, por favor?*" ("Ms. Paca, can I have one of lemon, please?")

In the evenings, Moms and my aunts sat with Grandma to talk and watch *telenovelas* while the *coquí* whistled in the background. Meanwhile, I'd be playing out front with my best friends, two brothers named Ofito and Danny. We'd be running around barefoot, catching lizards and shit like that.

Ofito was a chubby, dark-tannish kid with black hair who was about my same height and six just like me, a fun kid who also had his serious side. His little brother Danny was a stout, dirty blonde, five-year-old with a golden tan, a full-time joker, and if he wasn't laughing he was crying at full steam, angry that he couldn't get his way; the only time Danny was quiet and mellowed-out was usually at the end of the day when he was so tired from doing so much of both laughing *and* crying.

Sometimes I went with my father to my aunt's crib to hang out with my Uncle Rafi. He had his *marquesina* hooked up with a bar, a leather couch, and a large-screen TV. Even though my pops and Uncle Rafi were in their own world, having drinks, watching baseball games, and talking about things I ain't give a fuck about (I routinely zoned out and was never really listening anyway unless it was a boxing match), I used to go over there just because of how fly that *marquesina* was; I wanted one just like it.

Within six months, my parents were talking about moving yet again. This shit was getting played out; I was tired of the constant change of location, having to start over at another school and once again make new friends. But to my surprise we were only moving to the unoccupied house right next to ours. It really didn't make too much of a difference, but I was excited 'cause Ofito and Danny would now be my next-door neighbors instead of my two-houses-down neighbors.

My parents and theirs were good friends; one time they even took a weekend trip to the island of St. Thomas together and left us kids to be taken care of by our big sisters.

Ofito and Danny were the first long-term friends I ever had. Before them, it was basically my sisters for the last six years. Now I finally had some like-minded, mischievous accomplices to play with on a daily basis. We were almost inseparable.

But sometimes, I just wanted to be left alone.

One hot-as-hell afternoon, I was sitting by myself under a small palm tree that was on our front lawn, partially covered by its long drooping leaves, just lost in my thoughts. It's where I went for shelter whenever my skin was frying under the twelve o'clock sun. I can't recall what put me in those moods—it was probably my father—but I do know I didn't wanna be bothered.

After a while, Ofito and Danny came outside. I nodded to them but still kept to myself. They noticed I ain't wanna kick it with them and kept their distance, speaking to me from the edge of our driveway.

"*Oye, Gustavo, que te pasa?*" ("Hey, Gus, what's wrong with you?"), Ofito asked.

I just shook my head.

"*Ay, bendito, Gustavito esta triste.*" ("Ahh, poor thing, little Gus is sad."), Danny teased with a whine.

I didn't say anything, just stared at the ground.

"*Déjalo quieto, Danny. Ven, vamos a jugar, Gustavo.*" ("Leave him alone, Danny. C'mon, Gus, let's play.")

I shook my head again.

"*Míralo. Él va llorar como una nenita.*" ("Look at him. He's going to cry like a little girl."), said Danny.

He then picked up a rock and tossed it at me lightly like an underhanded pitch in schoolyard baseball. It hit the grass.

My body stiffened up.

My ears got on fire.

He threw another.

As usual, soon Ofito followed Danny's lead and they were both throwing rocks my way.

I ain't warn them or anything.

I just sat there letting my anger build up.

With that hot Puerto Rican sun on me, it was nothing but heat on top of rising heat, explosive lava about to bust.

47

The sweat trickling down my forehead was boiling.

I felt a heavy pressure between my temples.

After a few more volleys of rocks, I was ready to detonate.

My anger was concentrated on Danny since he was the only one talking slick and initiated the rock throwing. I knew Ofito was just trying to coax me into playing with them 'cause he was aiming at the grass around me. But Danny intended on hitting me; he was just easing his way into it by inching closer and closer each time he threw another one.

After he threw another rock much harder and it struck my leg, I snatched a nice sharp one off the ground, jumped up to my feet, and threw it at him with such force that it penetrated his skin and got embedded into his forehead.

For a split-second, Danny looked at me wide-eyed and dumbfounded. He then brought his hand up to his shiny tan forehead and felt the rock stuck there. Danny's facial expression turned to agony as he opened his mouth wide to scream and nothing came out at first.

Oh, shit.

I was mesmerized and startled by what I had just done. After about five seconds, that little motherfucker screamed like if I had cut him across the face with a box-cutter.

I felt my heart speed up with the quickness.

My father then ran outside to see what was going on, and on cue, I jetted past him and locked myself inside my bedroom. I just knew he was going to whip my ass with the belt. He ran in after me and tried getting me to open the door. I ain't budge.

I was paranoid.

My father's beatings were serious, and this time, I knew that even though he would understand I was just defending myself like he had taught me, he would still beat me down in order to stay cool with Danny's parents; Pops' M.O. had always been "Friends Before Children". If it had been some other people's kids, all charges against me would be dismissed immediately. But against his friends' kids, there was no way I would ever get a fair trial. Those were means for instant punishment by beatdown. Pops was getting ready to jimmy the door's lock with a butter knife when my mother persuaded him into letting her talk to me instead.

That was a close one.

My father's combat skills against his own children included punches in the head, kicks in the stomach, and faces being bashed into walls; not to mention belt-whippings, open-hand smacks, and a list of other shit I can't remember—most likely repressed memories caused by the severity of the violence he inflicted on me; some shit you just don't wanna remember.

Now, don't get me wrong. I wasn't an abused child; at least I don't think I was 'cause they weren't prolonged beatings. But he did shit to us that no parent should to do their children. Do something that irritated him, and you'd get one of three things in return: a scream, a combination of two of the things I already mentioned, or something new like a karate chop to the collarbone. Actually, screams were definite and daily.

"Pa' que no salga maricón!" ("So that he won't come out a faggot!"), was Pop's excuse for his over-the-top spankings. That was something a lot of idiot fathers used to say to their sons, not realizing that they were probably doing them more bad than good with that verbal abuse, turning healthy kids with no psychological issues into hateful, confused homophobes in the long run.

According to him, boys needed to get hands put on them to toughen them up. Yeah, right; that was just a bullshit excuse. Beating his kids was just what *he* needed to get his stress off.

I later apologized to Danny, but he was never the same around me again; he didn't laugh as much and was kinda subdued most of the time. That rock in the forehead humbled him; he became more serious and curious, finally acting like the youngest in the crew, asking Ofito and me questions to learn things from us. I wasn't proud of what I had done to him, but this new Danny was something I could get used to; I should've done it sooner.

Shit Iz Real

My father had kept renting that first house we lived in on the block to use it as his personal warehouse. Merchandise was piled up in every room, stacks of boxes full of canned foods, snacks, and beverages. Unlike New York City and Connecticut, my father didn't have a bodega in Puerto Rico; instead he was a supplier to mad grocery stores and supermarkets throughout the island.

Pops would hustle anything he could.

I remember once he even had a couple of life-sized statues of African tribesmen that he was selling. They used to creep me out. There was one of a kid my size with a bone through his nose; I used to lean in to look in its eyes and wonder if it could come alive while we were sleeping like the little voodoo doll in *Trilogy of Terror*. Then I used to get outta there in a fuckin' hurry.

Man, I loved Puerto Rico. At the time, the lovely palm trees and hot weather became a symbol of where I wanted to spend the rest of my life. One thing that was really dope was that the school days were shorter. There were two schedules; either you went from 7 AM to 12:00 PM or 12:00 PM to 5 PM. Five hours and you were outta there! Who *wouldn't* wanna live there?

At breakfast and lunch, you were pretty much served the equivalent of a home cooked meal—rice and beans and chicken—with a tall cup of chocolate milk. In the states, you got the chocolate milk, but it was always in a little carton that left you with a cardboard-like aftertaste on your tongue. Later in life, I realized that a tray of food served in a New York City public school wasn't much different than what was served in its jails.

There was a lot of fly shit out there.

Places like *El Yunque* were off the hook with rivers and waterfalls that we played in, a long stretch from the concrete corners and brick buildings that would surround me for most of my life. Whips looked like Matchbox cars; you might see a red Corvette with a yellow design across the side that looked like an upside-down hockey stick, or a navy-blue Monte Carlo with baby blue and white streaks on the hood and trunk. The music coming out of them and being played at strip malls and people's homes varied from Salsa—especially The Fania All-Stars (you know, Willie Colón, Héctor Lavoe and crew)—and old school *Jíbaro* tunes, to Soul and Disco. Barry White and Love Unlimited

Orchestra's "Love's Theme" was on all day every day. You couldn't go anywhere without hearing that shit.

During that first holiday season on the new block, a group of us kids got together at nighttime to sing Christmas carols in front of our neighbors' decorated homes. It was supposed to be a one-off. But then people started coming out and blessing us with some change (mostly pennies and nickels; quarters were like "Whoa!") and pieces of candy. Some of them stayed and enjoyed full songs, even making requests, while others rushed back indoors and turned off their lights as a hint for us to go the fuck away.

That didn't stop us; we thought we had found a way to make some money. I guess you could say singing was my first hustle. At the end of the night, we probably split like a buck-fifty between ten of us. We kept it going for a couple of more nights until more lights were being turned off at the sounds of our voices and finally nobody else ever came out to greet us.

After I found out Three Kings Day—which was also my mother's birthday—was celebrated only two weeks after Christmas, and kids received just as many presents on it, I was convinced Puerto Rico was paradise. I remember getting a Green Machine—the Rolls Royce of Big Wheels tricycles—and riding up and down the street mad early that day, attempting to do a 360-degree turn like the little white boy in the commercial.

My parents definitely came through every year on those holidays, blessing all four of us with a bunch of gifts. I had no complaints. From the outside looking in, everything must have seemed like it was perfect for my family; we had two homes on the same block, Pops ran his own business, we dressed decent, ate good, had almost everything we wanted and were happy. But it really wasn't; there were things happening that I was too little to notice, understand, or even pay attention to.

My father was the cause of all the bullshit. It was like he was dead set on destroying his own family. For one, he liked to spend more money than he made. Then he had to scramble and hustle his ass off to catch up on the bills. That alone caused tension and arguments. As if that wasn't enough, he also drank excessively and sometimes disappeared for whole weekends, a pattern he had started back in Connecticut. Maybe my mother thought moving to PR would change things but shit only got worse. Pops probably lost his mind when he saw all those Iris Chacon's and J. Lo's on the island and was gone fucking a different one every time.

Recently, he had also begun treating Aggie real fucked up for no reason at all, harsher than the rest of us.

It was too much things going on. I could only imagine the stress Moms was going through at that time. Even though she was good at hiding how she really felt, and usually was the type to avoid conflict and resolve problems peacefully, one night I saw her lose it.

It was a Saturday. My father had taken Cookie and me with him to a festival in Dorado; no carousel rides or Ferris wheels, just mad food, music, liquor, and big booty bitches. Pops spent the whole time—from mid-afternoon into the late night—flirting and dancing with women.

You would think he forgot we were even there. I mean, he occasionally looked for us and made sure we ate and were alright, but mostly he was having a good time doing his own thing. Back then, we didn't pay any attention to that; we were just excited about having so many other kids to play with without being supervised. But once it got dark, the other kids started leaving. Me and Cookie were exhausted and ready to go home, but Pops just kept saying, "Yeah, in a little while", as he continued drinking and chasing ass through the rest of the night.

"Yeah, in a little while." That's a game he played well into his seventies; Pops tried to keep you hostage whether you were with him at one of his hangouts—a bar, bodega, or any *negocio* owned by a friend— or you visited him at his crib in Queens; you almost had to fight your way out every single time.

Finally, past two in the morning, my father used his drunk-driving skills to swerve us through the darkness and get us home safely.

I walked into the house half-asleep, kissed my mother—who was standing in the kitchen waiting for us—and headed straight for my room. As I changed into my pajamas, I could hear my parents softly arguing in the kitchen. The volume went slowly escalating until I don't know what my father said to her, but whatever it was made my mother flip the fuck out.

"Te voy a matar!" ("I'm going to kill you!"), my mother yelled, so loud that the whole neighborhood must have heard it.

My sisters and I ran out of our rooms. I stopped in the dining room, shocked by what I saw: my mother had my father pinned down on his back on the kitchen countertop, her left hand holding him down by his throat while her right hand was raised overhead with a hammer in a tight grip, my father squirming and struggling to seize that arm and keep her from bashing his face in, which had a look that defined absolute fear at that moment.

My mother's eyes were rolling into the back of her head; it's something I only witnessed a few times in my life, but whenever it happened, we all knew to shut the fuck up and put our heads down, even as adults. There had been two other incidents that I remember clearly where my mother got like that, and if you asked her about them, she couldn't recall them ever happening; I guess she used to black out when she was really pissed the fuck off.

"*Te voy a matar!*"

"*Nooooo, Emilia!*" my father pleaded, looking as if he was drowning, trying to keep his head over water, desperate for life.

"*Te voy a matar, Armando!*"

"*Nooooo! Por favor! No he hecho nada mal! Es que te has vuelto loca?!*" ("Please! I haven't done anything wrong! Have you gone crazy?!")

"*Loca?! Hijo de la gran puta! Yo te he dicho a ti que no te lleves los niños contigo en tus borracheras!*" ("Crazy?! You son of a bitch! I told you not to take the kids with you on your drunken binges!")

That's when I knew my mother had lost it. I had never heard her yell or curse before. But right then she had called my father one of the worst curse words ever, *hijo de la gran puta*. People say it means "son of a bitch", but it really translates to "son of the grandest whore". I had learned it from Danny. That little dude could be a pain in the ass when he wanted to, but he taught me a few things, specifically Spanish curse words.

My sisters Aggie and Leticia were able to stop Moms from totally snapping and committing murder that night, but things never really got better between my parents. Moms was old school, though; she believed in trying to keep the family together no matter what. And she still loved my father. Or at least she thought she did.

In early 1978, while Héctor Lavoe was singing his heart out on the stereo in our living room, shit got worse. In one of his reckless and drunken outbursts, in front of guests that had been enjoying themselves, my father's monstrous side came out.

"Si no fuera por mí, estuvieran trabajando de dos cuartos separados!" ("If it wasn't for me, you'd both be working out of two separate rooms!"), Pops screamed, insinuating that my mother and Aggie would have become prostitutes if he had never come into their lives. Pops had his episodes of nastiness when sober, but liquor was beginning to make him beyond vicious.

He then crushed Aggie's feelings further. *"Yo ni siquiera soy tu papa!"* ("I'm not even your father!")

Aggie was devastated; she kinda knew it already, having heard it through the whispers of cousins who thought cruelty was fun when adults weren't listening back in Connecticut. But my mother had kept that secret from Aggie for seventeen years.

Nah, Moms ain't sleep around or nothing like that; my father wasn't even close to being in the picture at the time of Aggie's birth; he was still trying to figure out what to do with himself throughout his first few weeks in Miami. It was just that Moms had completely shut out the existence of Aggie's father so that he would never be mentioned, 'cause it all brought back too much pain, a pain she didn't want my sister to live with, the same pain she had lived with and held inside for all those years.

Mama Used to Say

Moms had been born and raised in *el campo,* the countryside town of *Corozal*, a mountainous region of Puerto Rico made up of farms, dirt roads, and wooden homes that were all a good distance from one another. She lived in a tiny two-bedroom house with an outhouse deep in the backyard.

While living in Puerto Rico, we visited that abandoned, worn-out house and got an idea of how they lived. What they called their backyard, I considered a jungle; there was even a bull roaming around freely back there. My mother explained how they all used to gather around a little battery-charged radio and listen to soap operas after dinner before they even had any television. There was no electricity, candles gave them light, and they used a stream by Grandpa's farm to bathe themselves.

My mother was the sixth child born to my grandparents. Altogether, Grandma had given birth to eleven children, nine girls and two boys (the third, oldest brother and a few other sisters were by way of Grandpa). Women back in those days raised families the size of football teams on the regular; I imagine she must have pushed the last ones out as easy as taking a dump.

My mother's two brothers died young; a baby boy born just before my mother had gotten sick and died at eleven months old. Her teenage brother died while Moms was still a little girl in the 1940's; he was crushed under Grandpa's pick-up truck after it flipped over in an accident.

When it happened, Grandpa was stuck inside of the upside-down vehicle because the metal stick shift had gotten lodged into his forearm. But when people that were trying to help him get out told him that his son was pinned under the back of the truck, he tore his arm up to get himself loose. Grandpa ran out all bloody to try and save him, but it was already too late.

Now, you can say it's ironic or just a coincidence, but Mom's brother had just finished hiding in the back of the truck unbeknownst to Grandpa, just as I had done in *my* father's car years later. I had no knowledge of him until I was in my thirties.

School was my mother's first love. Learning and solving new problems was always an exciting challenge, an away-from-home adventure, something fresh compared to the "same shit, different day" daily routine at the house.

Don't get it twisted; Moms had a beautiful home life, but school brought her into a whole other world of arts, cultures, and sciences besides just math and reading, plus it was a way of meeting new people. Some of her classmates lived close by; others had to hike miles to and from school.

But just after turning fifteen, midway through her freshman year, my mother's high school days suddenly came to an end.

The reason for that was a boy.

One afternoon, my mother and some of her sisters were out on their front porch talking about how their day was at school. Their older brother's girlfriend Rosa was with them.

Just then, a kid they all knew was walking up the hill, passing by on his way home from school when he stopped to say hi and catch a breather. The kid was a high school senior with plans of leaving to the military that summer after graduation. Since he lived further up the mountain, he had passed by hundreds of times before, but that day Rosa figured she'd have some fun with it. She later told my grandfather that the boy mainly engaged in conversation with my mother, like if he was kicking it to her.

Grandpa took my mother out of school the very next day.

See, that was some old school chickenhead shit; Rosa knew how strict my grandfather was but still thought it was amusing to stir up some trouble anyway. Moms lost out on getting a full education in Puerto Rico 'cause of that bullshit.

Less than a year later, tired of the boredom from being stuck at home every day and not doing anything else, Moms asked Grandpa's permission to go live in New York City with a few of her older sisters; since the mid 1940's, one by one they had all been gradually leaving the island for the big city life. She really didn't expect him to let her go; how the fuck would he let her leave the country if she couldn't even leave the house to go to school, right? Bullshit. Grandpa said yes. He understood that there were more opportunities for my mother in the States.

Her first few months in New York, my mother lived on 27th Street and 6th Avenue in downtown Manhattan. She later moved to Washington Heights, a quiet uptown neighborhood with a zero crime rate in comparison to the years that I grew up there.

Back then people didn't hang out in front of buildings or on street corners, they instead gathered at neighborhood parks; any congregating on sidewalks was brief. They occasionally went to ballrooms for a night of dancing, which were nothing like the clubs of the 80's and 90's that I used to go to where people got shot and stabbed on a regular. Women dressed elegantly in beautiful dresses with their hair done, men wore neat suits and were clean-shaven. Some shit straight out of *West Side Story*.

My mother wasn't no slouch; right away she enrolled in the evening classes at George Washington High School to learn English while working days alongside her sisters at a factory.

To further explain the difference of how the neighborhood once was, I'll relay a story my moms once told me of when she lived on 176th and Audubon Avenue in 1956:

My mother, two of her sisters and a friend or two, would stop after night school to chitchat a little more on their block before going home. After about fifteen minutes, a tall Irish police officer patrolling his designated area would routinely walk up to them, tap on his wristwatch with his index finger, and politely say, "It's getting late, my friends, time to say good night." Everybody went home without a fuss and the next day was another good one.

Fast-forward thirty years later, and the calm, peaceful streets of Washington Heights had become a chaotic, murderous and drug-infested flea market.

On October 5th, 1961, my mother—a beautiful, kind, intelligent, and caring woman of twenty years young—gave birth to her first child, Agnes. Moms had dated Aggie's father for a short time but fallen in love with him mad fast; they even had a portrait taken of themselves, him in a brown suit and Moms in a radiant pink dress; you can look at it today and see the love on her face screaming out brighter than any color on the drawing itself.

But even with all those good qualities Moms had, there was one thing that was an issue: her skin color.

Aggie's father was a pale white Cuban with blue eyes. He struggled with the possibility that his own mother back in Cuba wouldn't accept my mother because of her tan complexion, so he left her as soon as he found out she was pregnant. Moms bounced around from living with relatives of his to the home of one of her sisters throughout her pregnancy, probably still hoping they would get back together. Meanwhile, Aggie's pops moved to Ohio, married a white woman, and had three kids with her.

When Aggie's pops first left, Moms was living with my aunt *Titi Mari*. She still hadn't told her that she was pregnant or that she smoked cigarettes. One day while stressed out, puffing on a stogie somewhere nearby and wondering what the fuck she was going to do, *Titi Mari* caught her smoking and reprimanded her. Being that my aunt was already overbearing as it was, my moms was scared to tell her about the baby in her belly, so she used that busted-smoking incident as an excuse to move out.

The rest of the story goes that Moms somehow hid her pregnancy from most of her sisters, and by the time she gave birth she was living with my *Titi Sylvia* and her husband, *Tío Juan*. Moms shared the bed with my aunt and uncle. With no money for a crib and nowhere else Aggie could be placed to sleep overnight, they had to get creative. So, they took a drawer out of the dresser, put it on the floor, and my Uncle Juan's flight jacket was used for padding. Every night they'd put my sister—wrapped in her baby blanket—inside of it. When Uncle Juan got up to go to work in the morning, the first thing he did was take Aggie out and put her in the bed with Moms and my aunt.

So, yeah, Aggie's first bed was a drawer.

On October 5th, 1966, Aggie's fifth birthday, her father was in town and was supposed to go meet her. Moms must have been going through a bunch of emotions and real excited regardless of what had happened between them in the past; the important thing was that Aggie was finally gonna meet her father.

But it never happened.

Nah, he didn't run off a second time like all those other cowardly deadbeat fathers of the world; that might've been better. Instead, he was stabbed to death, either in the stairway or the elevator of the hotel he was staying at, just as he was on his way to see her. The hotel was near the old Loews Theatre in my hood, which means that my sister never got to be embraced by her real father by only a matter of blocks and minutes. Some said it was a robbery, others said it was a woman that did it.

Nightmares

As beautiful as Puerto Rico was, it had its dark side.

One time they found a man chopped to pieces just a few blocks outside of our community. Word had it that his gay lover didn't like the fact that he was ready to move on. Chopping his dick off wasn't enough, though; dude was sliced and diced like a pig at the meat market.

We had this main road called Dr. Diego Alvarez Chanca that connected all the little communities around the way. My street was called Dr. J.G. Padilla. As a matter of fact, nearly all the streets in my hood were named after doctors. They must have been some real good ones to get that kind of recognition.

Anyway, Dr. Diego Alvarez Chanca had a bay next to it. At the middle, there was a small bridge for people to cross over to the hoods on the other side. Instead of being thrown in the water at the bay, the dead man's body parts had been placed in a small space under that walkway. I remember the stench of his rotting corpse in the air; every time you hit that main road it punched you in the face and stayed there for a while. Not even closing the car windows could keep that shit out; that smell was nasty as hell. After a few days, it was what led to him being found. Wasn't nothing all them good doctors could do for him by then, though.

Another time, after going out to buy a carton of ice cream with Moms one night, a car began following us as we walked along that main road. The bodega was a good eight blocks from our house. Apart from the occasional car driving by us, Moms and me were the only people outside. It wasn't too late, maybe around eight-thirty at night, but that strip was mad dark and quiet. The bay where they found that chopped-up guy was on the other side of the street.

As we walked back home, a long, four-door sedan began trailing behind us. It must have been going about two miles per hour. I can't recall if it was too dark to see or if the windows had tints, but I looked back to scope it out and couldn't really tell who was inside; I could only make out the silhouette of two people, the driver and a passenger. While my mother was totally unaware of it—probably lost in her thoughts thinking about all the turmoil my father was causing her—I noticed it right away but didn't say anything to her until we got to the end of block.

"Mom, that car is following us."

After catching what I had just said, my mother glanced over at the car only once and simultaneously tightened her grip on my hand. She didn't say anything, but I could feel she was terrified. We walked a little bit more and then turned into the street that served as the only way in and out of our neighborhood. It was a short block.

At that next corner was the house of *Los Mercedes*, a huge family that lived in the biggest house in the area. Since a bunch of their family members were hanging out in the *marquesina*—including Mr. Mercedes and two of his grown sons—my quick-thinking mother rushed us in to say hello; she was hoping to mislead our pursuers into thinking that was our home. Moms had figured nobody would wanna mess with a family where there were a couple of men present. She made small talk with the Mercedes clan, I think she even told them what was going on, and after watching the car slowly cruise down to the next block and turn the corner, that was our chance; Moms abruptly said her goodbyes while we were already on the move and we ran down the block to our house before the suspicious car got back around in time to see us.

I hurried inside the house to catch the rest of *The Incredible Hulk* while *Mami* stood by the doorway in the *marquesina* telling Aggie about our stalkers.

"No te gustaría verme enojado!" ("You wouldn't like to see me when I'm angry!"), Dr. Banner cautioned some dude.

Every time that show came on I used to watch the little nerdy guy's mouth closely and be like *what the fuck?* I thought the Hulk really spoke Spanish, but was confused about how his mouth wasn't moving with the words coming out of it.

"Ay!" my mother yelled. *"Esos son ellos!"* ("That's them!")

The sound of glass crashing the floor followed her outburst. Moms had been so startled by the mysterious car driving by that she dropped her bag of groceries, causing a bottle of milk to crash to pieces on the *marquesina* floor. See, she had thought that after circling that other block, those men would leave the hood and not come down our street. But she was wrong; they were definitely on the hunt.

I rushed off the plastic-covered loveseat to look through the living room window blinds. The car did a U-turn at the cul-de-sac and slowly passed our home once again. I watched it until it was finally gone and the block went back to being as still as a polaroid picture again. My eyes darted right to left.

Grandma's house.

Titi's house.

Nothing moving.

Years later, my mother told me kids were being abducted in Puerto Rico a lot back then. She believed they were out to kidnap me that night. But I always thought that incident could have turned out ugly for both of us.

My father wasn't around when that happened, and it wasn't because of one of his weekend disappearances either. Even worse, he had gone back to live in New York. I don't know if they had broken up; he and Moms' relationship was really bad in those days. But as a little kid, I was told that Pops left because his distribution business was falling off, so he decided to go back to NYC to get on his feet again. At least that's the story I was told.

69

But *Papi's* departure was way too sudden. Maybe there was more to it. Maybe he was scared that my uncles and cousins might get at him for what he had done to Aggie. In one of his violent outbursts, he pushed her to the ground and made her hit her head so hard that she wound up getting knocked out. Only a few days later, he picked up all his shit and bounced. But who knows, maybe the real reason he left so fast was a combination of both of those things and even more. I'm not sure if it was in his plans for us to come live with him or not. Maybe he was gone for good.

Sometimes I wonder what growing up in Puerto Rico would've been like, would I have ended up some college-educated doctor, lawyer, or successful businessman with a suit and tie, or was the street life in the cards for me no matter where my life took place, would I have been under that same one hundred degrees of sun in my Lee jeans, BVD, and Kangol hat burning the fuck up. Some things are just meant to be.

But Moms didn't like driving, so staying in Puerto Rico wasn't an option; only a few months after Pops left, in the fall of 1978, he and Moms worked it out and we reunited with him. We all stayed with the family of one of his closest friends—Cookie's godfather, Turi—until he could find us an apartment.

Aggie didn't come with us. She moved into her best friend's house and stayed behind to finish school. She wasn't trying to put up with my father's bullshit anymore anyway.

But Aggie's frustration by way of Pops wasn't over yet.

One day two men showed up where she was staying at asking where my father was. He owed them money. Nobody knows what it was for, whether related to his distribution business or something else, but Aggie said that by the way those guys looked—rugged, stone-faced individuals—my dad had to be into something bad. Maybe. Or maybe he just bounced with a couple of G's he owed for all that merchandise he used to get up front. Shit, maybe Pops only robbed a few hundred dollars for his trip back to New York. But whatever the fuck sneaky shit he did, in the end, Aggie had to pay for it. Every week she had to give those men more than half of the little money she earned from her part-time job at a supermarket. It was that or suffer the consequences.

As soon as she graduated high school, Aggie returned to New York to live with our aunt, *Titi Marí*. She never spoke to my father ever again.

I didn't understand what the fuck was going on, but it ain't really matter to me anyway; same father or not, Aggie was still my sister one hundred percent. I never gave it any thought to what having another father meant to her; I just knew she wasn't getting along with mine.

Broken Language

At first, I didn't remember New York at all. I could feel I had been there before, but ain't really have any memory of it. I was excited, though. Looking at those big buildings, the traffic of cars zooming by and so many different kinds of people in the streets, made it a place I was anxious to explore. And when winter came around and it snowed that first time, it was a wrap; I was hooked on the city. It was cold as fuck but so fuckin' dope at the same time. That skin-cutting cold air ripping my face apart was what snapped me outta my New York memory loss. As far as I could tell, nothing had changed since my toddler days. Back then it seemed like every time it snowed it was an all-out blizzard, leaving the hood blanketed in several feet of snow almost as tall as I was. *Shit*, when the snow piled up against cars and buildings, it *was* taller than me. And at eight years old, that was still the case.

My parents enrolled me into PS 132, a fortress of a building compared to the schools in Puerto Rico; *those* looked like small cottages. The size of One-thirty-two was overwhelming at first. It took a little getting used to. Going through those spacious hallways and multiple staircases felt like hard work the first couple of weeks. Even though I spoke perfect English, I was automatically put in a bilingual class only because I had just moved back from Puerto Rico. The majority of my classmates ain't speak a word of English. Some had no interest in learning it. The few that did speak it either had a fucked-up accent or spoke it so well that they sounded like fuckin' robots.

PS 132 had two schoolyards, one on either side of the building. After lunch, we'd go outside for the rest of the period. Right away, I clicked well with the Latino and Black kids from other classes who spoke English just like me. A few of the kids from my class didn't like that; those shifty-eyed motherfuckers occasionally glared at me and my new friends from the corners of their eyes; they had turned that language barrier into a reason to distance themselves from other kids. I didn't give a fuck. I still made a whole lot of friends anyway. What's really fucked up is, when I passed to the fourth grade, I was put in a bilingual class again and had to spend another year with those losers.

A lot of the kids I played with hailed from the Bridge Apartments, a row of four buildings that have thirty-two floors apiece and are based from Wadsworth to Audubon Avenues. There wasn't anything else like it in the hood. They were never called "the projects", but they were the closest thing to projects that Washington Heights had; the Bridge

Apartments were occupied almost entirely by Black families. My homeboys who lived there were kids with names like Carl, James, Durrell, Thomas, Julian, and the brothers Sean and Melvin.

I occasionally saw some of the kids from my class—Jose, Juan, Pablo, Ricardo, Jose, Pedro, Juan, Joaquin, Jose, and Juan (this ain't no joke, I even knew a bunch of brothers and cousins who all had the name Juan incorporated into their names in one way or another; Juan Jose, Jose Juan, etc.)—being picked on or made fun of by a few of the kids from "the Bridge". They got fucked with 'cause of their broken-English accents, their own foreign language, and the way they dressed—high waters and shit like that. I kinda caught on that for some of them that's where their dislike for the Bridge kids originated from, but I still couldn't figure out what they had against me; was I guilty by association, or was it something else? Not that I gave a fuck, but those cats gave me the cold shoulder all the way into adulthood.

Almost all the teachers were white. Whether it was Irish, Italian, Jewish, or whatever, they were white. White with red freckles. White with black beards. White with blue eyes. White on white. White. The only Latinos I remember working at the school were the bilingual teachers, one for each grade, and maybe one token Latina in the main office or as a school aide.

Oh, yeah—and Jose, the Puerto Rican janitor.

Jose was a thin, light-skinned dude with shoulder-length, dead black hair parted down the middle of his head and a scruffy Dr. Fu-

Manchu-styled mustache. He mostly kept to himself, but every now and then, he greeted the students with a head nod and a "What's up, shorty?"

After school hours, when all the teachers were gone, Jose would still be there working until the early evenings. This is when I would see him sitting out on the schoolyard steps taking a break with a joint in his mouth and a beer in his hand—Budweiser. Jose always had good words of advice like "Stay in school, man" or "Hanging out in the streets don't get you nowhere, shorty". No matter what knowledge he dropped, he always ended it by shaking his head and saying, "You don't wanna end up with a job like this", looking like he regretted the path he had chosen in his own life. I respected his words of wisdom and appreciated his concern, but I didn't really know what he meant 'cause the allure of the streets hadn't snatched me yet. Still, I wish I could find him and shake his hand today, 'cause now I see that if I had gone by his simple advice, it would have saved me from going through a whole bunch of unnecessary bullshit.

After Jose stopped working at One-thirty-two and faded from the neighborhood in my mid-teens, I can't recall any other men ever encouraging me to do something positive with myself. They either offered me no advice at all or wanted me to carry guns or sell drugs for them. I was never told that going to prison or dying was a definite for most of the kids that lived that life. It was almost as if the pitfalls of doing crime were one in a million, something you didn't have to worry about.

Our principal, Mr. Finkelstein, was a pale, broad-shouldered man with a full head of white hair. The expression on his face was stern; he never even grinned. When I first heard the term "cold blue eyes", I could honestly say that thinking back to Mr. Finkelstein's glare was what defined that for me. Whenever he walked into the schoolyard, everybody froze. If he caught you running, he'd say, "Hey, sonny", and signal you over to him with his index finger. Then he'd poke you on the forehead and say, "No running in my schoolyard" before pointing at the wall, which meant you would have to spend the remainder of the period standing against it, while all the other kids continued playing and running after Mr. Finkelstein went back inside.

The ladies whose job it was to watch us during recess used to sound like characters from *The Sopranos*. They were gangster grandmas who were nice but respected because they didn't hesitate to put you on the wall either. The most feared one was the tough-looking, chain-smoking, gravelly-voiced Mrs. Weiss, a hefty bespectacled woman whose face reminded me of an owl; if you fucked up, she'd grab you by the arm and scream your head off. Other than that, the actual teachers were laid-back. The music man, Mr. Katzman, occasionally got pissed off and slammed the piano shut, but I can't blame him; we were some badass kids. He only made us laugh harder with those tantrums, though.

There was only one nutcase in that school: our Science teacher, Mr. Fulton, a tall man with reddish skin, brown hair, an intense look in his eyes, and a strict, nasally tone of voice. He was feared even more than Mrs. Weiss because his physical abuse was on another level.

"Pedro, what is the scientific term for water?" Mr. Fulton asked.

"H...Two-O?" Pedro quietly replied with a question more than an answer, scared of having it wrong.

Mr. Fulton would then go into a deep dark place. His eyes were absolute madness at that moment as he approached you and gripped the sides of your head tightly with both hands, lifted you first out of your seat, and then up off the floor altogether to make you face him, shaking you violently through it all while your feet dangled in the air.

"Well, is it?! Is it H2O?! Weren't you paying attention to today's lesson?" he asked, his voice now trembling with anger.

I saw him do that to a lot of kids.

One time, Mr. Fulton started to approach *me* with that crazy look and I snapped him right out that shit.

"If you touch me, I'm bringing my father tomorrow."

Mr. Fulton stopped dead in his tracks. He was shocked. I guess nobody had ever challenged him before. He took a step back, cleared his throat, and then turned to continue teaching the class. He glanced at me a few times as he spoke, but after that day he never tried that bullshit with me again.

That I know of, nobody ever reported him. Kids were afraid to tell their parents about it 'cause it was believed you could never win against a teacher. We looked at it as though they ran the show; they were adults, we were kids, and that was that. Even though we weren't guilty of anything, we believed that challenging anyone in a position of authority would only get us in trouble with our parents. This kind of mindset also applied to the police; they did dirt and we never said anything about it. So, when cops in the hood started getting wild a few years later, they got away with assault, robbery of drugs and money, and more shit on a day-to-day basis. Murder, not as much, but they did that too.

Just like a little kid talkin' big about cash
thought he was runnin' game but they stole his whole stash

Big Mouth

When we moved back to NYC, my father had somehow already opened his own restaurant right there in the hood, two blocks away from where we were living. That shit was dope for the fact that every morning on the way to school, I'd stop off for some breakfast—Cuban buttered toast and a cup of coffee—and then come back after three o'clock, eat an official Cuban sandwich, wash it down with a Pepsi or Malta, and chill. I'd hang out in front of the restaurant a lot just watching the world go by.

Pops was real good at getting a business up and running, but as soon as he saw the money start coming in, he always found a way to fuck it up; he used to leave his restaurant unsupervised all the time so he could go drink with friends and probably chase hoes. He also liked to brag too much, and one time got robbed of five G's for it.

One afternoon in the early spring of 1979, Moms and *Titi Mari* took me and my sisters to "Jew Park", a sprawling park where old folks played chess, teens and young adults got busy in handball, and kids like myself fucked around on the monkey bars and slides and ran across the open space of pathways and grass and enormous rocks, and wound up on the raised tarmac full of benches that gave you a perfect view of the George Washington Bridge, which connects New Jersey to New York City only four blocks away on 178th Street, one of the main routes for Jersey drug dealers to come cop weight in the hood by the mid 80's.

When we came back a few hours later, the apartment door was open a few inches; somebody had broken in and ransacked the apartment. Turi's rent money and jewelry were gone. But that wasn't all. The intruder knew exactly what he was looking for and where to look: the tall drawer in my parents' room. All of my father's pairs of socks lay unraveled on the bed; that's where the grand prize was originally stashed at, but that bitch-ass thief ain't find it there. I guess maybe Moms had some type of funny feeling that day 'cause she had moved it before we left. It didn't matter, though; that burglar even searched through my toys on the closet shelf and discovered the five G's inside my Shogun Warrior box.

See, my father was the type of person that always had to let the whole world know what he had, and he usually exaggerated his shit. He later admitted to my mother that he had opened his big mouth about having that money stashed for another business venture. He had shared that info with a guy he barely knew, a customer having coffee inside his restaurant. Me knowing how he liked to stretch the truth, my father probably said he had ten thousand stashed. I bet the guy then used Jedi mind tricks to fill in the blanks of where exactly the money was hidden.

With the guy sitting on a stool and my father standing behind the restaurant counter, the scenario probably played out something like this, but in their Spanish lingo of course:

"You need to be careful," the future thief advised, "they've been breaking into a lot of apartments lately." He probably even went into one or two stories about people he knew and what got robbed from their homes as if he really gave a fuck. If he was talking about some real shit, it was he himself that robbed them.

"Yeah, I know. Shit ain't easy out here."

"I like to hide my money in places thieves won't ever think of…like a box of cereal…or in the oven. You gotta be creative with it."

"I wrap it up in a pair of socks. No one's going to think of looking inside a pair of socks." Pops was cocky about it.

"That's a good one, I never thought of that." the thief lied.

"Of course, who's gonna take the time to look through all of your socks?" my father replied even cockier than before.

Right there, the slick son of a bitch's job was halfway done; he knew where to look. Then he went in for the kill.

"You gotta be careful, my friend, especially because you're a restaurant owner."

There it is: he spit the magic phrase—My Friend—to gain my father's trust and confidence. He had probably been spitting it for months, *amigo* this, *amigo* that, working on Pops from day one. Poor Pops ain't even see it coming.

My Friend—it's supposed to be one of the most comforting things you can hear come out of a person's mouth. It symbolizes trust. But where I come from, it's one of the deadliest terms used. My boy Gangsta B usually said it when he was getting ready to shoot you.

"True, this neighborhood ain't what it used to be."

"I imagine you take a cab home every night after closing, right?"

"Nah, I'm not that far. I live right there on 180th. I walk home every night. But I always got my piece on me." Pops bullshitted. Or not. But he definitely fucked up by telling him where he lived.

That was way too easy. Now all the burglar needed to do was send someone—preferably a young fine female—to follow Pops into our building; besides his occasional hangout missions, he went up to the crib a few times a day, whether to take money, take a nap, or take a shit, and closed shop about eight at night, not too late for a chick to trail him to the block either.

Since Pops was a natural flirt, he probably made her job easier, making her feel welcome to follow him. She then entertained his friendliness with small talk and went up to the same floor as him. Hopefully, she got paid a couple of extra dollars 'cause it was an asthma-inducing fifth-floor walk-up.

Pops stopped at our door to pull his keys out and exchange a few more words. She knocked on one of the other three doors as a front. He put on his silky-smooth Elvis Presley wannabe tone of voice to say,

"*Adios, mi amor*", before walking in and closing the door behind him. The lady then took a mental note of our apartment number, turned around, and bounced before our neighbors even answered their door.

Too easy.

After that it was just a waiting game; they watched who my father came in and out of the building with, learned who were his acquaintances and family members, and waited for the apartment to be empty so they could hit it.

My father was a fool.

See, this all started with him trying to run game on dude, trying to impress him by talking about his money. But in the end, dude ran game on Pops and took it all. It was a chess match my father lost from the very first move he made. And dude had been patiently waiting for it all along.

That shit may have happened any another way, but there's no doubt that the customer Pops had bragged to was the one that did it; he was a regular at the restaurant right up until the burglary. After it went down, my father never saw him again.

9mm Goes Bang

Summer 1988.

Nah, his brains aren't all over the place; they're still inside his head. He's a piece of artwork left on the concrete he had once smiled on so much. His body is still warm, which means he was just smiling here just a few minutes ago. Now he's gone. Or he might be in another dimension but at the same time standing here with the rest of us, just watching as the homicide detectives make jokes and laugh as they examine his corpse. I've always seen him as a happy-go-lucky kind of dude, a positive person. What the fuck could he have done to piss somebody off to *this* degree? He was so full of life; his smile was contagious; now he's motionless, in eternal sleep. Thirty years will pass and his vibrant smile and a hole in his head are the only things I will remember him by.

My Block

About a month later, I went with my parents to check out an apartment for rent in a huge building at the corner of 183rd Street and Saint Nicholas Avenue. Building 600 took up half the block. My new elementary school, PS One-thirty-two, took up the other half. In front of its main entrance was the 34th Precinct. The idea of having a police station right around the corner probably made everybody in 600 feel like it was an extra safe block.

We walked inside, and I was stuck; I had never been in anything like it. The building lobby was immaculate, a fucking palace. The intercom was on the left-hand side before a second set of doors that led to a bigger part of the lobby. Those doors and the partitions on their sides were made of a steel designed in the shapes of flowers and plants, all encased in glass from both sides. The floors, walls, and a fake chimney near the center were all made of marble, or something like it.

There was a wide, wall-sized mirror near the mailboxes. 600 even had an elevator.

Hell yeah! No more walking up those five flights of steps at Turi's house!

But just in case I was in a hurry, there were two staircases, one beside the elevator and another behind it. That second one was sneaky; if you weren't familiar with the building, you wouldn't even know it was there; the perfect place for rapists, stick up kids, and home invaders to lay in wait for victims once the crack era started rolling in. Both staircases took you up past six flights and ended in an L-shaped hallway space that had two separate exits. Building 600 was so big that it had two rooftops.

As we got off the elevator on the third floor and looked for apartment number 38, I noticed the hallway had three sections with three apartments apiece. At Turi's building, it was just a small square with four doors on each floor. Apartment 38 was down the longest & narrowest part of the hallway.

An elderly German-Jewish couple was still living there, packing their belongings and getting ready to move. To my young eyes, they were like two hundred and something years old combined. Their home resembled an antiques museum; everything sparkled from spotlessness but looked like it had been around since or before 600 was even built— 1920.

After they gave us a thorough tour of the apartment, it was a no-brainer; with three bedrooms, a long hallway, and windows facing the front of the building, my parents knew it was the spot for us. They signed the lease the same day.

Building 600 had one thing that really distinguished it from almost every other building in the hood: the apartments that ended in the numbers 8 and 9 had a unique fire escape; instead of being a regular set of stairs outside of a window, it was a spiral staircase on the outside of an extra door in the first bedroom. I only saw one other building with a fire escape like that, one that I used to get away from a police raid later in life. Each apartment also had a built-in safe in one of its bedroom walls. I bet my father loved that feature; he probably thought about how his money would be way safer there than in a pair of socks.

Two weeks later, right after the old school crew moved out, 183rd became the block I would love for life.

A bunch of kids from all types of backgrounds lived in my new building. At that time, that shit was like the United Nations. The sixth floor had the Puerto Ricans Bighead Benny, Erin and his half-Black little brother Keane, a funny Ecuadorian named Joe, and Michael Black—a Jamaican kid who eventually learned to speak Spanish from hanging out with so many of us Latinos for so many years. Tabolan, a Black kid on the fifth-floor, was the most intelligent and humble of them all. He was only twelve and was already almost six feet tall and talking about college. Little Jay, the second youngest after Keane, lived on the fourth floor in the apartment above mine; he was Dominican. On the second floor, another Puerto Rican, Edwin, and a Haitian-looking Dominican who went by Boogie, rounded out my first 183rd crew.

There were a lot more kids in my building, including Jewish and Greek, but the Jews weren't allowed to play with us. It ain't help that we made fun of their little hats; this one freckle-faced, blonde-headed kid made it a habit to run by us every day at a hundred miles per hour, probably so we wouldn't fuck with him. The Greeks were always down, though. A bunch of them were from down the block on Wadsworth; the two buildings next to the 34th Precinct were nothing but Greek from top to bottom.

Later additions to our crew were Raul, Chu-Chu, and Flat-face, kids who didn't last more than two or three years on the block.

Even one of my classmates lived there. But just because of his inability to speak proper English and my relationship with those who did, Ricardo never got cool with me. At least that's why I thought it was. He always put on a mad face and looked the other way whenever we crossed paths in the street. Homie had put himself in a self-imposed segregation. Only time he ever spoke to me was if he was desperate for an answer no one else around could give him. It wasn't too many interactions; he'd just come ask me some shit like once a year, usually when I was chillin' on the corner, sitting down on the building poles.

1982.

"Have you seen Boogie?" Ricardo asked, looking awkward like *Damn, I really didn't want to talk to this guy.*

"Nope."

1979.

"Did you do the homework Mr. Junco gave us?" he asked, half-angry, half-curious. Probably hadn't done it yet.

"Yup."

1985.

"Jose is making too much noise in the hallway!" Ricardo complained to me as if I was the building super, his grill stained by a staring-into-space stupidity mixed with *I'm mad!*

"I ain't his father. Whaddayou want me to do about it?"

After those exchanges, Ricardo would say nothing else and walk away just as sudden as he had stopped, looking like it had hurt his pride to have had to talk to his Puerto Rican classmate and neighbor. But at that time, I didn't think me being a Puerto Rock had anything to do with it; I actually didn't dwell on it at all. As far as I could tell, all us Hispanics were the same. I thought we were all just a bunch of kids whose parents came from different countries where Spanish was spoken. I didn't see any difference in our features, our accents, nothing. I was blind to all that at least into my late twenties.

Even as grown-ups, after they did learn enough English, I never saw him or any of his buddies—two other angry kids from my third-grade class—associate with anything but Dominicans. While everybody else absorbed a little something from all the other cultures in the hood, they avoided it as best as possible like it was a sin; Washington Heights was the melting pot of all melting pots back then—food, music, and more shit from all kinds of nationalities at your disposal. But those guys ain't want no part of it—probably wouldn't even eat a Cuban sandwich if it was for free; they should've been the ones to trademark the FUBU name-brand, *For Us, By Us*, 'cause they wasn't fuckin' with anything else unless it was absolutely necessary.

The corner of 600 would become my main chill-out spot, a place where you could find me over the next twenty-five years kickin' it with my homies, lighting ants on fire, playing tag, smoking blunts, guzzling forties, packing a nine millimeter, three-eighty, or sawed-off shotgun, spitting game to fat-ass shorties, spitting rhymes to my block brothers, selling weed, trying to lure drug dealers from other cities into the building so I could sell them cocaine and crack on a triple beam scale— or stick them up, or just sitting there by myself watching the people and cars go by.

The hoods of strangers' parked cars and the poles outside the building were where I chilled at—block furniture. "The poles", as we called them, were these thick metal poles only certain buildings had surrounding them. Not sure why they were put there, maybe to prevent out-of-control cars from crashing into buildings, but they looked like they were meant for people to chill out on—except for the ones on other blocks that were smeared in tar or had the little sharp monster teeth across the top to keep everybody off. But that shit ain't stop the hangouts; there were more than enough cars, milk crates, and other block furniture on every block for people to sit their asses on anyway. *Shit*, the steps at building entrances were comfy as fuck.

On one of my first days there, I was chillin' on the poles by the building stoop, just checking out my new location when a pitch-black, skinny kid walked up to me. He looked just like one of those African statues my father had in Puerto Rico. All he was missing was the bone through the nose and the yellow and black African garb. No lie, he looked like it so much that it was as if the statue had come to life and followed me to New York. I was mesmerized by the resemblance.

"Hey, whussup, man? Are you new in the building?" he asked with a friendly smile, and then extended his hand to shake mine. "I'm Boogie."

Boogie was like an all-star sports expert around the way, real good at everything he played, always rounding up other kids in the hood for games of baseball, football, basketball, stickball—anything played with a ball. He was the quarterback, pitcher, referee, umpire, and coach all in one; there wasn't any position that he didn't know how to play. Easygoing and funny, the only times he got mad was about shit that was sports-related. Boogie was good peoples, though, one of my best friends as a kid.

That day, as we hung out on the building stoop, Boogie pointed out his stepfather to me as he entered the building, a quiet Cuban man in his fifties. The thing that stuck out to me the most about him was a baseball-sized lump he had on his throat. I never asked Boogie what it was, but a year later I found out what a tumor was when he died of cancer.

Within another year, another Cuban man moved into Boogie's house. A short, grouchy alcoholic with a mean temper and a PHD in Fuck All of You, Cheo was nothing like Boogie's previous stepfather. While you never heard a peep coming out of Boogie's apartment before, now it was an all-out war every day between Cheo and Boogie's mom. Boogie didn't involve himself in that, though; he never even complained about it. I guess going outside to play sports was an escape for him. It probably kept his mind off what was going on at home for most of the day.

Cheo would be in and out of the building all day and night to buy beer, never had enough of it. He'd stand on the corner for short periods of time and curse out the people walking by. Then he would make his way to the front, stand by the entrance, and harass female tenants as they passed through. I don't know how he didn't catch any ass whippings in those early days on the block, but in the long run, he'd pay for all his bullshit.

One week after meeting Boogie, I came across Bighead Benny and Michael Black in the schoolyard on 182nd Street. At the time, I didn't know they lived in my building.

It was a Friday, one of those late afternoons where the sun was halfway down, peeking out from the back of the hood, and the sky was reddish, a mix between an orange Crayola and a splash of Kool-Aid. A couple of Black guys and girls in their late teens and early twenties were sitting on a platform by the school windows just hanging out—quite a few Black families lived on that block until the mid-eighties. In the evenings, an older crowd of mostly Blacks and Puerto Ricans gathered at both schoolyards to smoke weed, drink forty-ounce bottles of Old English 800, and talk shit while playing music on their boomboxes.

Teddy Pendergrass: "Turn Off the Lights" (1979)

I was looking for someone to play with when I wandered into the schoolyard. Bighead Benny and Mikey were messing around with a huge puddle of water, fishing out an empty soda can with a stick or something like that.

"Whussup!"

Benny: "Hey."

Mikey: "Whussup."

I don't know you, nigga was written all over his face.

"Can I play with you guys?"

Bighead Benny was with it. "Yeah, c'mon."

Under his breath, Mikey was slower with his reply. "Yeah, you can play with us." But the scowl on his face said a flat *No.*

"What are your names?"

"He's Whitey." Mikey said with a mean grin as he nodded towards Bighead Benny, obviously referring to his skin color.

"He's Blackie." Bighead Benny blasted back with a laugh.

Bighead Benny and Mikey both were two years younger than me, but we were all about the same size, except they were heavier 'cause of their chubbiness.

"Whussup, Whitey. Whussup, Blackie." I waved, trying to keep the jokes rolling. I thought that would break the ice but instead it nearly got my head broken. While Bighead Benny laughed, Mikey flipped out and turned into Bruce Lee on me.

"What did you call me?!" Mikey then took a quick look at the Black teenagers and twenty-somethings behind me.

"Blackie. He's Whitey…and your Blackie, right?"

"What?!" He glanced at them again. "See, now I gotta kick your ass, motherfucker!"

Mikey came at me and began throwing spinning back kicks one after another. I kept myself about a foot away from his dirty Converse sneakers with my hands up for protection as I walked backwards in the direction of the schoolyard exit. After each kick missed me, Mikey's eyes shot back over for a split-second before he threw another one; he was trying to impress them.

By the time we were passing right in front of the audience he longed for, Mikey was out of breath, off-balance, and looking sloppy. All kinds of shit was on his face: worry, fatigue, he was huffing and puffing real hard and feeling stupid after having thrown like twenty kicks and missing with every one of them.

Heatwave: "Groove Line" (1977)

"Yo, leave that kid alone, shorty!" one of the older guys who was named Tyrone shouted.

At that point, Mikey stopped and turned around to walk back towards Bighead Benny and stumbled a little to the side, dizzy from all that spinning he had done. He then caught himself and continued walking, exhausted and hunched over with his head down looking like a little junkyard dog.

I walked back home feeling fucked up—mad, embarrassed, and confused. But I was disappointed more than anything else because I really wanted to make some new friends around the block. I had already been back in New York over three months and still hadn't run the streets with other kids; I was anxious to explore the city with some new Ofito's and Danny's.

So, on Saturday afternoon, I decided to give it another try. I came out of the building, and as I walked down the little hill to the schoolyard on my side of the block, who else comes strolling out of it and my way but Mikey.

Not him again.

Mikey looked like any other little kid—humble, in his own world—until he noticed me. He then clenched his fists, got mad-faced, and started walking faster like a little man on a pissed-off mission. I made like I didn't see him and scanned the schoolyard for other kids. It was empty. I stayed on my course down the hill and didn't turn back like he probably expected me to; we were like a cool little choo-choo train and a hotheaded locomotive about to collide 'cause Mikey and his Jackson Five afro were approaching fast. When he got within five feet of me, he put on his Billy Badass talk again.

"You got away from me yesterday, chump! Well, today—"
BOOM!!!

I punched Mikey in his chubby cheeks crazy hard and shut him up with the quickness; his words fell to the sidewalk in pieces. A continuation of nonstop punches followed. I had never fought before in my life. It felt good. Pops had always told me to hit motherfuckers back, never stay hit. It's the one thing I can say I remember him teaching me. But the beating I was putting on Mikey was probably a reflection of the aggression Pops had been putting on me for the longest. The only other time I had struck back was when I pushed Danny's wig back with the rock in PR. But this time, to be the one giving out the punishment with my own hands felt good. Left hooks. Right hooks. Footwork. Body blows. Lethal combinations. Sounds good, but I was most likely just throwing a flurry of bullshit punches. Watching all that boxing since diapers probably helped me out, though, probably molded what my brain was orchestrating my hands to do.

It felt good.

My hands were too fast for him and Mikey never really got a chance to fight back. I was determined to play that day, and if I had to beat him up for it to happen, I was motivated to do so.

After a thorough ass whooping, Mikey yelled, "Alright, alright! You win!" and I stopped hitting him.

I stepped back away from him, and after he got himself up, I nonchalantly asked, "You wanna play with me?"

Mikey adjusted his t-shirt, gave me the perplexed *this kid is crazy* eyes, and quietly replied, "Sure."

Until this day we're the best of friends. But back then I felt like that first beatdown entitled me to bully him whenever I wanted to. Those first few years on the block, I used to bang his head against the radiator pole in the hallway and beat him up every now and then. I was lucky Mikey never fucked me up; he was a real strong kid with rough, heavy hands, hands of stone like Roberto Duran; he could punch a concrete wall with all his might and it didn't even faze him. I had him showing

97

other kids that specialty of his all the way into high school so that nobody would ever fuck with him. But that was only the half of it; it was also my way of making them realize that even though I was a bony, weightless kid, I had one strong motherfucker with me.

I soon met the rest of the crew.

Erin was a cool kid but a goddamn show off. Whenever he got a new pair of sneakers, he did something outlandish to make sure you saw them. Like one time, he jumped on the hood of a car and did some bullshit tap dancing; another time, he randomly started doing handstands. It was all about getting his feet up to eye level, so you could notice them. He'd do this kind of shit until somebody mentioned the new kicks on his feet.

"You could stop that bullshit already, Erin. We saw your new Nikes a long time ago. Do you want us to get a microphone and announce it to the world?" Mikey spit.

Erin also had the "I'm The Super's Relative" complex. Since his stepfather's father, Henry, was the building super, Erin felt like he owned it and could lay down the law sometimes. It was like that all over, though; a lot of the building superintendents' family members in the hood thought they were block royalty.

"Henry doesn't want us playing in the elevator."

"Henry don't want us on the roof."

"Henry won't like if we…" was Erin's most used line when it came to a Henry regulation reference.

Fuck Henry. None of us said it out loud, but I'm sure that's what we were all thinking. All that Henry shit went in one ear and out the other. We all did what the fuck we wanted to anyway, including Erin. I guess he ain't really care either; throwing Henry's name around was just his way of trying to have some leverage over his big homies; Mikey, Bighead Benny, and me were all older than him, me the most by five years. The little cocky motherfucker was smart.

One thing about Henry: He was the greatest super we ever had, in his late sixties and busting his ass sweeping, mopping, scrubbing, and fixing shit throughout every inch of that building to keep it right. 600 went downhill fast after he left. But it wasn't just because of the crack invasion; those other supers and their helpers just ain't have the same work ethic as Henry. For a few, there were ulterior motives to why they took the job. Some of them *were* caught up in sniffing coke or smoking crack, or both. They catered to the incoming drug dealers as if they were high-profile tenants, participating in the bullshit by getting landlords to rent them apartments for the purpose of turning them into drug spots and stash houses and doing other favors for them. In turn, their hospitality was rewarded with drug freebies and money.

Every summer, Erin would go visit his grandmother in Co-op City up in the North Bronx and come back bragging like it was the best place on Earth. It was hard to believe a nice section of the Bronx existed. I didn't mind it, though; it always got me to reminiscing about the only paradise I'd ever seen thus far.

"Yeah, Puerto Rico's like that. It ain't got no garbage in the streets. There ain't no rats or stray cats either. It's even better, though, 'cause it got palm trees and it's never cold."

The sunny realm of Puerto Rico was all I could use to go up against Erin's concrete heaven and make it a conversation, or else he'd be the only one talking for like an hour. The other kids just quietly listened 'cause they hadn't been anywhere but the hood, the South Bronx, and maybe Times Square, and at that time, the hood was the nicest out of the three.

But in reality, Erin's description of spotless streets and a neighborhood full of doctors, lawyers, and other professionals driving brand new Beamers and Benzes, and living in condos in impeccable buildings that soared through the clouds, was nothing like Puerto Rico. What I really saw in my head was just about the same thing you see on the album cover of Ghostface Killah's *Ghostdini: Wizard of Poetry in Emerald City*, minus the yellow brick road and the bitches laying on the bright green grass and red roses. The way Erin amped it up, Co-op City made Washington Heights out to be as ugly as the South Bronx.

Erin's stepfather was a Black man named Lou, a hard-working electrician with the Homie the Clown bald-on-top afro. Every time I think of Erin's house, music and weed come to mind. While we played Atari 5200 in Erin and Keane's bedroom, Lou frequently passed through the hallway, smoking a joint while soulful sounds made their way from the living room into the rest of the house. Lou didn't know it, but he taught me a lot about music. Even though a lot of the same shit was playing in Connecticut and Puerto Rico, he was the one that really exposed me on a deeper level to Marvin Gaye, Barry White, Earth, Wind, and Fire, and a whole lot of other great artists. Soul was the soundtrack of that crib, playing in the background just about every time I was there over ten years. Nothing but good music and good memories when I think of their home; Atari games, fucked-up cardboard 3-D glasses to watch trashy 3-D movies on channel eleven, and the sweet smell of some good Mary Jane.

One weekend, when it was already hot and muggy outside, our doorbell unexpectedly rang past eight o'clock at night.

Pops wasn't home.

I followed Moms from the living room into the long hallway, curious to see who was at the door. Nobody really used to come to our house yet, none of my or my sisters' friends, especially after dark; Pops wasn't having that. My *Titi Marí* only came by on Saturday afternoons (and every other Sunday, all of us except for Pops went to her crib on 174th and Audubon Ave for dinner—my Italian Uncle Ralph's slamming spaghetti and meatballs—while he watched the Yankees beat somebody's ass on TV).

Moms twisted the two knobs on the regular locks, shifted the bar on the police lock to the right, and opened the door to find a three-year-old boy standing there by himself. I was next to her.

"Mi mami está ahí?" ("Is my mother there?"), he asked in a little raspy voice.

"No, mi hijo, tu mama no esta aquí. Donde tu vives?" ("No, son, she's not. Where do you live?"), Moms curiously asked.

"Ella me dijo que venia a jugar Bingo aquí." ("She told me she was coming here to play Bingo.")

"No, mi amor, ella no está aquí." ("No, my love, she's not here."), Moms replied with concern as she looked down at the child. *"En donde tú vives?"* ("Where do you live?")

The little boy stared at me for a few seconds with a look of recognition, like if he knew I was from the world of children just like him, but only bigger. Actually, I'm not sure; his look could also have been interpreted as *what the fuck is you looking at?* I, on the other hand, felt like I was looking at a little man. Since I didn't have any younger siblings, it was the really the first time I had encountered a kid his size since way back in kindergarten. His composure and the way he communicated himself made him seem a lot older than he really was.

He looked back at my mother and said, *"Pero ella dijo que iba adonde Rafaela a jugar Bingo."* ("But she said she was going to Rafaela's to play Bingo.")

"Como tú te llamas?" ("What's your name?"), I asked.

"Yo me llamo Jose." ("My name is Jose."), he replied, fully aware that he had just made a new friend. The little dude was sharp.

"Y donde vives?" ("And where do you live?")

Little Jose gestured with his hand for us to follow him. He led us upstairs to apartment forty-eight where he lived with his mother and two older sisters. It turned out he had gotten confused; when he snuck out to go looking for his mother, he ended up at our apartment below instead of the one he'd been to before, the weekend Bingo spot above at apartment *fifty-eight*.

Jose's mother, Venecia, came by the next day to thank Moms for getting him back home safely.

Moms greeted and made small talk with a few other ladies in the building, but Venecia was the only one that she truly became friends with in all the years that we lived there. They'd visit each other from time to time and talk over a cup of coffee, but their bond really formed on our living room windows. Ours had a little balcony just big enough to put a couple of plants or sit and enjoy the view of the 183rd and St. Nicholas intersection. It's where Moms sat and smoked her stogies at day and night. Venecia would lean out from her own window overhead, and that's how they usually kicked it and hung out together the first few years.

Jose ended up being the little brother I never had. Because of me, he got out of his house and was exposed to a lot of stuff at a real young age. Venecia trusted me and let him go with me to the pool, movie theatre, parks, and all those bangin'-ass block parties the summers were flooded with. We had all those things within a few blocks, but what our mothers didn't know was that most of the time we were exploring outside the neighborhood, going to Times Square for movies, Van Cortlandt Park's pool in the Bronx, and the massive Fort Tryon Park a mile away.

By the time Jose was ten, Venecia let him go with me to house jams around the hood. Our mothers thought we were at innocent birthday parties in well-lit homes, rocking birthday hats, singing *Happy Birthday*, when in fact, they were dark festivities full of gang members and drug addicts, my age and older.

After midnight, Venecia and Moms might as well have had binoculars; they used to make those windows and the little garden balcony look like a prison watchtower as they waited hours for us to come home. A few times they went looking for us after two in the morning but never found us 'cause I was slick enough to never give exact addresses, only wrong street numbers.

A few short years after meeting him, and after Hip Hop rushed into my bloodstream like some uncut heroin in the vein of a dope fiend, I felt something had to be done to distinguish this Jose from all the other Jose's. So, I started calling him Little Jay.

Games People Play

During those first five years, my friends and I—including our little homeboys from neighboring blocks—were all over the place; instead of just being confined to 183rd, we'd play games like *Freeze Tag* within a four-block radius.

After getting tagged, some of the more gullible kids tortured themselves by staying in those frozen positions for long periods of time, no matter where it was; a basement, a stairway, the roof, it didn't matter. One time I saw Edwin from the second floor frozen in a running stance on 181st Street, dozens of shoppers walking around him while he waited to be tagged back into the game. We had forgotten about him and were playing a totally different game when he finally resurfaced about an hour later.

Not me, though. If more than two minutes passed and the coast was clear, I cheated my ass back in.

We also played *Superheroes and Villains*, a game we invented in which all of us chose the super powers of two comic book characters for combat. With *Wolverine's* unbreakable bones, accelerated healing abilities and sharp claws, and *Juggernaut's* unstoppable force, I was damn near unbeatable.

My superhero ass-kicking methods were fierce.

"Hah, I got'chu! Incinerated you to ashes with my—"

Erin was mad hyped up until I dropped the bomb on him. "Nah, man, I was transparent! You forgot who I am today?"

Sometimes I switched out *Juggernaut* for *Vision*, a weirdo in a green and yellow suit that could shoot lasers out his eyes and control his gravity by turning as solid as a rock or as light as air, so light that his body turned see-through and shit just went through him like he was a fuckin' ghost.

"Nah, man, that's bullshit! You didn't see me coming!"

I threw my right fist out, stopped at his throat, and stuck my imaginary claws through his fuckin' jugular. "Wolverine claws!"

Erin's face was blank.

"Fuck *you*, Johnny Storm!"

I then looked at Erin's belly.

"Vision eye lasers—tearing all the chubby off your tummy! Ahh, man! The hotdogs you ate for lunch are all over the floor! There's even pieces of shit there!" I laughed and kept fighting the real hardcore cats like *Spider*-Man, *Colossus*, and *Iron Man*.

The Human Torch ain't shit.

For that game, we stayed on 183rd. The rooftops of both our building and the social security office on Broadway were within bounds. That one had an accessible stairway on the backside of the building that took you right up to the top of it. Nobody ever fell from either one, or from the fire escape with the spiral staircase at 600; we used it to run down from the roof all the time.

Dodgeball was the shit back then. Several games jumped off throughout the day in the schoolyard. The older guys from 184th, like Chino and other Uptown Crazy Crew members, would engage in Crazy Dodge Ball—every man for himself. Some of them were fully-grown men with at least five times our strength, but me and my boys still played with them anyway.

Those games were intense. I got hit with a combination of the jitters and an adrenaline rush for however long I was able to last in them. It was fun watching the smaller kids, mad quick on their feet and death-defying, diving out of the way of oncoming attacks from those big guys. Even better was when kids caught a fuckin' cannonball to the chest and hugged it like it was their sweetheart; it would sting like hell and send them flying back on their asses, but at first they were too excited to even feel the pain—they were just fired up about catching the ball and getting one of those bigger motherfuckers out of the game. It was like a heavyweight boxer being blown away by a flyweight. That shit made them instant celebrities to those watching the game, the Michael Jordan's of Dodge Ball, even if it was just for a day.

"Ooooooh!" a couple of people would shout.

"Oh shit, that little nigga caught your shit!" someone would yell, while the player that got ejected from the game walked to the sidelines pissed off, looking like *Fuck that little nigga!*

Right after the little kids got back on their feet and took a shot at another player, you'd see them rubbing their burning chest while getting back into survival mode. A few of them were constantly targeted by headhunters 'cause of their natural ability to stuff those body shots with ease.

The worst part was when a gangbanger got his hands on the ball and annihilated a kid with a shot to the face at close range.

Ouch.

Everybody in the schoolyard cringed as if they all could feel the pain, and in a way, they really did; it was that rush that went through the core of your body, that electric sensation, that mind-blowing feeling that lasted like a minute, that shit you felt in your chest when you saw the sudden decapitation of a child.

"Ooooooh!"

"Damn, shorty, he almost took your fuckin' head off!"

I saw a lot of tough kids hold in their tears, their faces with expressions like they had to take a shit. Unless they were really dark-skinned like Boogie, their faces stayed cherry-red for a long while as if they'd been in the sun too long.

It's too bad these games were never recorded; they were classics. I used to think Dodge Ball should be a professional sport without protective gear. They could've had little leagues, major leagues, official hood tournaments and all that. Yeah, a few of them might have ended in shootouts and a couple of deaths, but I bet it would've made for some good television, though.

Since the majority of the kids I hung out with were from the sixth floor, that was our headquarters when we weren't playing outside. They put me on to a lot of things up there, among them the New York City blackout of '77 and the Son of Sam serial killer. Those were crazy stories, but there was one that really stood out because it happened right on our block. They used to say that just before I moved in, an eight-year-old boy had jumped out a fifth-floor window thinking he could fly—after watching the movie *Superman* the summer before. Serious shit for me to hear since I was eight at the time myself. I used to look up at that window where he supposedly had jumped from, and then down at the courtyard where he landed in front of the spiral staircase, trying to picture it happening. *Fuck, that's a long way down.* And then I'd see a Puerto Rican kid I had never before seen in my life lifelessly sprawled on the concrete, somebody my mind conjured up on its own. See, for me it was a gift and a curse having such a creative imagination; I got so used to making myself envision how certain fucked-up incidents went down, that these days I still see things I don't even wanna see 'cause my imagination has no boundaries and does whatever the fuck it wants at times.

There was always some form of mischief going on, kids doing what kids do, but on some New York shit.

From the sixth-floor, we'd spit through a small opening down the stairway handrails so that people could get saliva on their hands off the railing. It always jumped off as a challenge to try and make your spit make it to the first floor. If you'd mastered your aim good enough, you might get it down to the second or third; the thicker the spit, the better; phlegm was a godsend. But even if it landed right below on the fifth floor, it really didn't matter; the real reward was catching a victim. It never too took long to see a faceless hand steadily sliding down the rail and eventually wiping the spit right off. That was usually followed by a rant that started with a *Shit!* or a *Fuck!*

Me and the fellas always busted out laughing loud enough for them to hear us and even got chased a few times. That's when the second staircase and the spiral fire escape on the rooftop came in handy the most. They never caught us. But karma was a little bitch since early in the game 'cause I myself got some nasty-ass slobber smeared on my palms numerous times.

The elevator was big entertainment for us, sort of like a ride at Coney Island. A few of us took turns riding on top of it once or twice and were quick enough to jump back inside in time to avoid getting crushed at the top. Sometimes, all of us combined at over five hundred pounds, would jump up and down while inside, making the elevator jerk left and right and bang against the shaft walls. We never made it get stuck between floors and needed the fire department to come rescue us, though; that kinda shit only happened to the people that weren't doing anything wrong in it.

110

But for nearly a decade, we did ring the hell out of that alarm on whole trips from One to Six and vice versa for no reason at all.

The elevator was a fuckin' playground. If more than four of us got on it, out of nowhere someone would yell "Corners!", and then everyone struggled to get one of the four elevator corners for themselves. Whoever remained in the middle caught a beating until he could force someone else out of a corner and take it for himself. The assault would then pass on to the next kid.

One time, our little Argentinian homeboy Flat-face was about to take some groceries up to his crib on the fifth floor while the rest of us were hanging out on the building stoop.

"I'll be right down to play with you guys."

"Ah-ight, Flat-face."

We watched Flat-face get on the elevator from the entrance and then we split into two groups and rushed up the two stairways two steps at a time, but quietly. We stopped on the fourth floor looking like a SWAT team that was getting ready to raid a fugitive's hideout—index fingers at our mouths, signaling each other to not make a peep. After we heard Flat-face go inside his apartment and the door shut, we stealthily invaded the elevator and took it up to the top floor. Bighead Benny, Mikey, and me then lifted Little Jay up to turn off the light bulb.

"Shit! It's hot!" Little Jay whispered as he tried to grab the bulb.

"Of course, it's hot! Hurry up, before Flat-face comes out and decides to take the motherfuckin' stairs!" Mikey replied.

Mikey was the first curse-aholic out of the crew, fully engulfed in filthy vocabulary before the age of seven. A good-mannered, respectful kid, but he definitely had some influence on the rest of us becoming junkies of what was considered by many old heads to be the language of the ghetto, not of the Heights.

"That's how the people from the ghetto talk!", some parents would say. And by ghetto, they only meant Black neighborhoods.

But if profanity had been crack, my sister Leticia was the one that handed me the vial and the pipe. Mikey was just an amateur next to her. With Leticia, it wasn't just about the words she used, but more about how the fuck she said them. She made cursing into a fuckin' art.

"Lick your fingers, Jay!" Bighead Benny franticly instructed.

Little Jay then did as Bighead Benny had told him and licked his fingertips in between small turns of the light bulb. I wasn't saying shit, anxious for the next part of our plan to come into effect. The light finally turned off just as we heard Flat-face coming back out of his crib. We then lay in wait in total silence as he pressed on the elevator button. The inside of it was tar black as it dropped back down to the fifth floor. The only sign of life was the mechanical humming sound it made.

It stopped.

Flat-face, nonchalant as fuck as he opened the door to step in, flinched in surprise when he saw all eight of our arms reach out and yank him inside.

"Wait, fellas!" Flat-face pleaded, "Nooooo!"

The elevator traveled up and down a couple of times while we beat his ass down. But shit, to keep it funky, that shit was more like a rumble; it was so dark in that motherfucker that we all caught a couple of lumps from one another.

Don't feel sorry for Flat-face. Animals were victimized on the regular, too. Uptown was flooded with stray cats back then. ("Before the rise of the Chinese takeout spots", some like to joke, insinuating they were all eventually eaten by the *Chinitos*.) They weren't easy to catch either. But one time, a kid named Kev was determined to settle the old debates of whether a cat really had nine lives and was it true that it always landed on its feet.

"Y'all been watching too many cartoons, man! A cat is like any other living thing; it can't defy gravity!" Kev argued.

"How much you wanna bet?" Leo proposed.

"Kev, why would they show that in all those cartoons if it wasn't true?! Heathcliff always lands on his feet! Top Cat always lands on his feet!" Erin reasoned.

"Don't forget Tom from Tom and Jerry, Erin!" Little Jay added. He was looking at Erin on some serious-as-cancer type-shit like if he had forgotten a real important detail.

"Yeah, that dumb motherfucker Snoopy's always bustin' his ass, landing on his head and shit." Mikey spit.

"How much you wanna bet, Kev?" Leo asked again with a little more enthusiasm. Leo knew the game of hustling real well while still at a young age, but it didn't translate into anything as an adult. By then he preferred sniffing coke over getting money.

"A cat cannot always land on its feet!"

"Yeah, I don't believe that shit either!" I agreed.

"How much you wanna bet?!" Leo yelled over everybody, growing impatient.

"I'll bet you a dollar!" Kev replied.

"Bet! Now let's catch one and see!"

The crew of six went on the hunt quick fast. After several tries with several cats, we finally caught one by the pile of garbage bags Henry had put out on the sidewalk. Kev immediately grabbed it by its tail and started swinging it over his head like a lasso. That fuckin' cat was screaming loud as fuck when Kev finally tossed it about twenty feet in the air.

Silence.

We all watched it descend while its body whirled in all directions and, right before it hit the ground, that fucking cat turned upright and landed on its feet in the middle of the street. All of us watched in awe as it effortlessly merged its landing into running and disappeared under parked cars.

"Gimme my dollar!"

"No way, that was luck! I didn't throw it high enough!"

"Bullshit!"

"I'm telling you, I didn't get to do it like I wannit to!"

"Okay, let's do it again! Two dollars! And this time we gonna throw it from the roof!"

"Fuck it! Let's go!"

Back at the garbage area, we caught that second cat much faster because we were all so anxious to see the outcome of it falling seven flights down. It was obviously a domesticated cat that had been thrown out recently; Kev got it to walk into his arms immediately after a little bit of that *here kitty-kitty* shit.

The ride up the elevator was on fire.

"Get those two dollars out'cha pocket, Kev, 'cause that cat is gonna shut you up!" said Leo.

"Yeah, right."

Meow.

"You really gonna throw it, Kev?" Erin asked.

"You damn right I am."

Meow.

"You gonna kill that fuckin' cat." I told Kev.

He just smirked and shrugged his shoulders.

I couldn't wait to see it happen.

Meow.

"Don't worry, Gus, it's not gonna die. It'll land on its feet." Little Jay aggressively assured me, serious as cancer again.

Mikey was in a corner quietly having his usual attack of the giggles, something he routinely experienced when committing some real lowdown mischief. He'd laugh uncontrollably until his chubby brown cheeks reddened, and his eyes got chinky and tears trickled out.

Once out on the rooftop, Kev didn't hesitate. After having calmed the meowing motherfucker down by petting it nonstop on the elevator ride, he tried to grab its tail, so he could twirl it like a helicopter blade and toss it, but it wilded out on him and dug its claws into his forearm.

"Fuck!"

Kev reacted by pitching it into the sky by one of its legs.

There's no way that cat's gonna live.

We watched that cat falling for what seemed like forever. We were only seven flights up above the ground, but it might as well have been the thirty-two floors at the Bridge Apartments. It looked like it was suspended in air, like it was skydiving, 'cause it remained in an upright position with all its legs spread out as it fell.

"I'll tell you what, no matter how that fuckin' cat lands, that motherfucker's dyin'! No nine lives for you, *Mr. kitty-cat!*" Kev joked.

"Yeah, that motherfucker's done." Mikey declared.

The cat finally hit the pavement.

"Ooooooh!" everyone but a dejected Kev shouted.

It landed on its feet except that its hind legs were at an angle like when a baseball player slides into home base. I don't know if it was injured internally and died later on, but at that moment, it ran off just like the first one did.

"Two dollars, please."

"*Unbelievable.*" said Kev.

Throwing a cat from the roof was nothing; during one July 4th weekend, I remember hearing that someone had stuffed an M-80 into a cat's ass and blew it to pieces around the corner.

There was no shortage to the fun we had; you could either find us on the block just playing *Skellies* or playing *Manhunt* at the enormous Fort Tryon Park a mile away without our parents' permission. We'd gather up fifteen to twenty kids—including Kaleem from 181st, Tony Tone, Carlito Boom-bow, Gromi, Ilagri, Freddy, Little Man, Pad, Junior, Kojak, Ant, and C-lo from 182nd, and Armando, Tomas, Larry, Ghandi, and Ariel from 184th—and be running the streets looking like a gang of midgets.

So far you heard of the elevator assaults and attempted murder of cats. Well, small-time robberies weren't off-limits either. Every now and then, I snuck a dollar out of my mother's purse for some candy, or to feed my addiction of playing a couple of rounds of Ms. Pac-Man at the Hobby Land toy store. But that shit got harder to do a few months after we got an ugly white Chihuahua named Tom-Tom. That little motherfucker used to bark like he was gonna tear me to pieces whenever I went near anything of my mother's, so either I had to abort mission or do that shit in a hurry, sweating and all that as if I was disabling a bomb in order to shut him the fuck up. Tom-Tom's retarded bulging eyes were always all up in my face, so soon other money-getting schemes had to come into play.

A loose parking meter on the block was once a heist target; a car had crashed into it and almost completely taken it out of the ground.

Throughout the years, it never got fixed and kids were always rocking it back and forth to pass the time, slowly chipping away at the already cracked cement that was holding it in place. By the time I was fourteen, Bighead Benny, Mikey, and me were fucking with it one day and we finally pried it out of the sidewalk.

"Yoooo!", all three of us yelled, surprised as fuck, but still trying our best not to be too loud so that if there were any adults around we wouldn't catch their attention.

We let it drop on the ground with a thud, Mikey went into his giggling attack, and Bighead Benny and I smiled down at it. All I envisioned was loose change and dollar signs.

"We finally broke it." Bighead Benny said, wide-eyed in amazement.

Bighead Benny, Mikey, and I had talked about what we would do in this situation; it was a scheme we had in the works for years, not that I believed it would ever happen. We looked around to see if anybody was watching and especially if anyone was at the building entrance. It was clear.

"Let's go!"

We then carried the heavy parking meter like a corpse into the building, onto the elevator, and up to the roof. We walked to the edge and tossed it over, dropping it down to an alley in our basement. We must've thought it was gonna explode and a hundred quarters would spill out onto the concrete floor like on some Super Mario shit. Instead, the meter stayed intact and put a dent in the ground. But we weren't ready to give up yet.

I went home and got a hammer.

All three of us took turns trying to break the plastic window on it, but that shit ain't get anything more than a couple of scratches. Shit was a waste of time.

"Damn! Now I can't go play no Ms. Pac-Man!"

Moms is like other moms, praying, holding her rosaries
It's been a week, where the fuck Pops is supposed to be?
his heart cold, somewhere below ze-ro degrees
Bounced for life & only left us a couple bucks for groceries

Looking at the Front Door

Pops' restaurant was on 181st Street, the mecca of shopping for everything except groceries in Washington Heights. I forgot the name of it, but my father still swears to this day that it was called Two Brothers, only because two Greek brothers sold it to him. The location was a jackpot. It was only a few doors down from Woolworth's and directly in front of Wertheimer's, the department stores of back in the day that served as our Target and Wal-Mart. One-eighty-first had three movie theatres: The Astral, which showed double-features, usually mixing one Spanish joint with an English one—a comedy and an action flick; The Heights XXX, a porn theatre, which I only ever saw one person either going into or coming out of nightly for as long as it was open; and the RKO Coliseum, our hood's premier movie theatre that showed the most anticipated new flicks first on gigantic screens inside of equally gigantic auditoriums. All three theatres were within two blocks from the restaurant, the porn joint was right around the corner. Mad stores occupied 181st Street and the nearby St. Nicholas and Broadway avenues; thousands of shoppers passed through my father's restaurant on a weekly basis.

Pops could have seen the millions he dreamed of if he had run his business the right way. But he didn't; he still spent more money than what he made. And it wasn't like he was buying some big, expensive televisions and things for the house, or a fly-ass whip. It was petty, spent entirely on the streets.

Don't get it twisted; our home was decent, refrigerator full, and he made sure our wardrobe and his jewelry was up to par, but the rest of my father's earnings went on partying—in other words, liquor and hoes. He wasn't getting crazy drunk or staying out on weekends anymore; in that sense he was doing good, being a family man. But he still had that itch for the hangout and lost a lot of money because of it.

All he had to do was hold on to that prime piece of real estate and shit could have popped off like he wanted it to. 181st Street is busier than ever these days. If he would have stuck around to teach me the business, we could have expanded and turned it into a club or a lounge. That block is the heart of Washington Heights.

After about a year and change of ownership, my father lost Two Brothers. But he quickly rebounded and opened another restaurant called Rancho Luna on 162nd Street and Broadway, a seedier, older-looking part of the neighborhood.

Nowadays, I sometimes wonder how my father got the funding for his restaurants and any other business ventures he got into. He didn't have any credit or a bank account, so getting a legit loan was out of the question. I'm guessing he dealt with loan sharks or borrowed dough from his Cuban connections. Up until the early 80's, it was mostly the Cubans who were running all the illegal business uptown, including the drug game. As far as Two Brothers is concerned, maybe he got his jump-start with that money he knocked off those cats in Puerto Rico.

Pops wasn't all bad; he could be loving and compassionate at times and was a comedian at heart, but he'd get furious at the drop of a dime, and it was beginning to happen more often without him even drinking any liquor. I don't know if it was that he was bipolar, or it was due to the financial holes he dug himself into. But whatever his issue was, he took it out on those closest to him. Maybe he just didn't want the responsibility of raising and supporting his kids anymore. Maybe it was too much for him. After all, then he'd have more money to spend on himself.

One night I walked into Cookie's room and she was stuffing some clothes into a book bag like she was going on a world tour.

"What'chu doing?"

"I'm running away."

"Whut?"

"I'm leaving, Gus. Dad is driving me crazy."

"What did he do?"

"I'm tired of him, that's all. He's always screaming."

I stayed quiet for a few seconds with images of Pops barking going through my head. No argument there; Cookie was right.

"Don't leave, Cookie…where are you gonna go?"

"I don't know. But I don't wanna be around him anymore."

I really didn't know what to say about Pops. I couldn't lie and say he was gonna chill and stop wildin' out on us anymore. I was worried about Cookie being alone in the streets. She wasn't one of those girls that were running around the hood hanging out. Not then at eleven years old or ever after that. It was a dangerous world out there for her—her, me, and anybody else I could think of, seasoned veteran of the streets or not; even the hardest of the hard got put to sleep on those streets sooner or later.

"Where you gonna go? It's dark outside. You gonna be alone out there. Don't go, Cookie."

My mind was racing on thin ice as I watched Cookie going from one side of the room to the other, grabbing her belongings and then finally slowing down and thinking about what I said.

"I'm just so tired of the screaming, Gus. That's all he does."

"Yeah, I know. But you have to stay with us; we're your family. Out there it could be worse. Where are you gonna sleep? What are you gonna eat?"

"I don't know." Cookie's voice dropped to a calmer tone. "I just don't wanna be around him anymore."

One morning, while sitting at the kitchen table waiting for *Papi* to serve us breakfast, my sister Leticia and I were laughing; I don't know what the fuck it was, but something had us rolling. We weren't being boisterous, just two kids quietly laughing amongst ourselves. *Papi* hadn't said a word from the moment we woke up; he was in deep thought while preparing some good shit over the stove. All of a sudden, he turned his head and looked at us like "What the fuck are *they* laughing at?"

"Cállense!" ("Shut up!"), my father barked at both of us, but he was really concentrating his anger on me.

Apparently, we didn't stop laughing fast enough for him.

Papi shocked the shit out of me when he impulsively snatched one of his *chancletas* off his feet and slapped fire out the whole side of my face, hitting me so hard that he knocked me off my seat. I got up from the tiled floor just beginning to cry but that cry automatically became a hysterical laughter when I again looked up at my father. A steady flow of tears still streamed out of my eyes, but I couldn't stop laughing. The thing is, when my father used to get mad and yell, his eyes popped out like Rodney Dangerfield's, so I couldn't help but crack up.

"Les dije que se callen la boca!" ("I told you to shut your mouths!"), he yelled again.

Leticia and I just kept laughing. *Papi* screamed at us again and again but was only looking at me as he did. We eventually calmed down and ate breakfast in silence. With the sensation of flames still burning freshly on the left side of my face, I then zoned out into my own thoughts and wondered why my father only hit me and not Leticia.

Does she get to laugh at the table 'cause she's fourteen? Damn, I can't wait to be a teenager.

I was confused at the time, but later I'd understand that Leticia was my father's favorite, even though that still didn't justify him smacking a three-alarm fire into my face.

Leticia was my father's first child with my mother. He had another daughter, Irma, from a previous relationship. I only know her from pictures. They say my father used to bring her over to our house back when I was a baby on 178th Street, but after my family relocated to Connecticut, he basically abandoned her.

Pops didn't play when it came to Leticia, though.

One time, he was driving his van by the block when he saw her walking home from school just minding her business. Just then, this scrunchy-faced older teen by the name of Cheeze—he had rolls on his forehead and his beady eyes, wide, mashed nose, and inflated bubble lips were all too close together, looking like his head had been put in a vice contraption—ran up and grabbed my sister's ass with a slick smile on his face.

Boy, did he pick the wrong time to catch a feel.

"Hey!" my father yelled.

Cheeze ran off.

Pops gave chase in his van.

Cheeze ran up Wadsworth Avenue and was too stupid to run down any of the cross streets, so a few blocks up, Pops caught up to him. Pops stomped on the brakes, jumped out the van, tackled him onto a pile of garbage bags and pounded him out.

During my youth, that kid Cheeze was a cocky and obnoxious dude that liked talk down to the younger kids. But he never fucked with me. His whole demeanor changed whenever we crossed paths, as if every time he saw me he was reminded of that beating he got from my father.

Maybe not on behalf of me and Cookie, but as much as my father loved Leticia, you'd think he was gonna be around forever.

Wrong.

By the spring of 1980, Pops had lost his second restaurant. He then opened a small meat market down the block from 600—on 183rd and Wadsworth Avenue, the Greek block. The place was kind of secluded. It was on a lonely hill where there weren't any other businesses. Hardly anybody ever walked by. Since he couldn't afford to hire any workers, my father had no choice but to be there waiting for customers all day by himself. Unlike the restaurant, where my father could come and go as he pleased, now he was trapped and didn't have anybody to talk to. That shit must have been tough on him. I used to come by after school to help out and find him looking bored and depressed every time.

Two weeks after Leticia's fifteenth birthday, on August 15th, my father left to work and never came back home. He didn't leave a note. He didn't call. Nothing. (I found out as I was finishing this book that he actually did leave less than twenty dollars on the kitchen table for my mother to pay all the bills and feed us with. Pretty thoughtful of him, huh?) After going more than two days missing, we thought something

127

bad had happened to him. When my mother decided to check his hallway closet out of curiosity, more than half his clothing was gone. My father had snuck his clothes out of the house little by little during his last week with us. I guess escaping in search of freedom was a pattern of his—first Cuba, now his family.

You could say that when it came to running away, Pops beat Cookie to it, except Cookie was only trying to get away from Pops—Pops succeeded in getting away from all of us.

My father's sudden vanishing was hard on me.

Yeah, he put me through different forms of torture while he was around, like how in Puerto Rico at six years old, he made me sit at the dining room table in complete darkness for like three hours, thinking that making me stare at it would change my mind about eating a large bowl of some greenish shit that looked like vomit. But that was nothing compared to other shit he did.

In New York, he'd left me alone in his parked car dozens of times to avoid getting a ticket instead of just putting some change in the parking meter and taking me with him. The reason he did that was because traffic cops ignored cars that had people inside of them. Pops always took the keys with him, which means at wintertime I was left in freezing temperatures without any heat, and throughout blazing summers I had no air conditioner. To get some air, he'd tell me to only crack the window a little so that I wouldn't get stolen—while he went into pharmacies and variety shops to have coffee with storeowners, or grocery stores and bars to drink beers with friends for two or three hours at a time. It's no wonder I was such a skinny kid; that car was hot like an oven.

My father even verbally abused and degraded me by consistently calling me names like idiot and dummy. If he asked me for something and I didn't get it right the first time, he'd flip on me. Simple shit, like if he asked for a book in a stack of twenty, he expected you to automatically know which one he wanted; pass him the wrong one and you were a piece of shit. And even though I wasn't one of those hyper, out-of-control kids, I was calm and respectful, obeying my parents to the fullest, my father still felt a need to give me a tongue-lashing and put his hands on me for nothing at all.

But even through all of that, he was still my father; his good still outweighed his bad in my nine-year-old eyes. I still loved him and needed him in my life. Without him, it would only be a matter of time before I got lost to the streets. Yeah, his discipline was harsh, but in some twisted way I believe it could have helped keep me on the right path. Either that or it could have made me turn out to be a whole lot worse than I did.

"Eeny, meeny, miny, moe
catch a nigga by the toe
if he hollers let him go
eeny, meeny, miny, moe"

Erase Racism

We all gathered in close and put our feet in a circle to see who was gonna be it in a game of *Johnny Ride the Pony*. Looking down at the assortment of little kid's feet, the types of footwear varied. Adidas. Nike. Puma. Pro-Keds. Moccasins. Pony. *Chancletas*...and some nondescript shit from Carter's.

"Eeny-meeny-miny-moe, catch a nigga by the toe—"

"That's it! You're it, Mikey!", one of the other kids yelled.

"Get the fuck outta here! What'chu mean I'm it?!"

"You're it 'cause you're the only nigga here! Bighead Benny said, 'Catch a nigga by the toe!'"

Everybody including Mikey laughed, even though a glimpse of hurt and embarrassment showed in his eyes.

Every time the Fourth of July came around, as someone lit the ricocheting firecrackers known in the hood as Nigga Chasers, it was followed by the yell, "Watch out, Mikey! It's comin' right for you!" Being that back then you could get your hands on an arsenal of fireworks year-round, that type of verbal abuse went on for weeks before the holiday actually hit and long after it.

We said a lot of hurtful shit all the time; we just ain't know how hurtful it was. But that's what kids do, speak without knowing what the fuck they're saying, especially when they're being taught to be brutes by adults with a mentality not that much superior to theirs. Unfortunately, a lot of those kids became those adults and are the ones teaching that same ignorance today.

As for the N-Word, it wasn't really common in my hood until NWA—1988 to '89. After Ice Cube and the rest of them made everybody feel comfortable with saying it, every other rapper started dropping it in their rhymes. And that just made matters worse; all kinds of people that didn't even speak a word of any useful English, from toddlers to middle-aged men, started spitting it like it was all good, along with their other tiny collection of the language—Fuck, Shit, Fuck You, Motherfucker, Bitch.

In the Streets of New York

Every kid goes through that phase of hanging out with the older, more mischievous kids that put him or her up to a new level of troublemaking. Ant and C-lo were it for me.

They introduced me to 42nd street and parts of the Bronx I don't remember ever seeing with my mother—the bombed-out neighborhoods and people that wore poverty on their stressed-out facial expressions and bodies from head to toe.

On Times Square, hookers and drug dealers were all over the place. One cat would try to peddle heroin to us right in front of a movie theatre, and only a few feet away, another offered us angel dust in front of a Peep Show. There seemed to be dudes pushing all kinds of drugs after every other three or four establishments. Most of them looked like junkies themselves.

Not the hookers, though. Most of them were voluptuous women, healthy-looking stallions with incredible asses and huge, round titties. The days of crackheads with pussy for sale at five dollars a pop weren't among us yet. I'm sure plenty of them had their vices, but none of them looked like the skeleton whores that would hit the streets after '85.

"I got that Red Rocket, fellas. Five dollars is all you need." a man in a pair of raggedy jeans and a dirty t-shirt would say.

It didn't matter that the oldest in our group, C-lo, was only twelve; drug dealers approached us all the time anyway. We just ignored them and kept it moving. I felt kinda nervous about it at first. But those feelings were quickly pushed to the side by the thrill of being on a downtown mission with my little homies. After a while, we'd just laugh it off and say some stupid shit.

"No thanks! You take it! You look like you could use some more of that stuff anyway!"

Movie auditoriums were always smoky back then. People smoked weed and cigarettes inside theatres as much as popcorn was eaten; I probably got my first buzz at nine years old and didn't even realize it until just now. It makes sense, though, the way we used to come out of those places chinky-eyed and sluggish, everything looking surreal. I used to think it was just the effect of sitting in a dark theatre for up to five hours, but looking back on it now, I believe the marijuana smoke floating through the air was part of what made me feel that way.

Ant and C-lo were already smoking weed at that time, but they never did it in front of the rest of us; they'd just show up on the block blasted out of their minds. Other moviegoers were obviously drugged on stuff stronger than weed; you would either see them leaning over their seats with their eyelids barely open, mumbling to themselves, or erratic and restless, jumping up and down and screaming crazy shit at the screen.

"Kill that motherfucker! What'chu waiting for, bitch?!"

"*Shhhhhh.*"

"Shush, you, goddammit! How the fuck you want me to be quiet?! They about to kill that skinny white bitch! Are you gonna help her, motherfucka?!" After a short pause, "I didn't think so!"

Back then, it seemed like hundreds, maybe even thousands of more movies used to come out at theatres. And they were crazier; way more pussy and tits, mutilations, heads exploding, and serial killers than in the movies of today. Me and the fellas were hooked, especially on the horror flicks. We'd pay two-fifty apiece and sit through a double or triple feature every weekend.

That's when I started writing. I'd go home after the movies and write a ten-to-twelve-page story about my little crew being chased and massacred in disgustingly creative ways by a masked killer, who always wound up being brutally killed himself by the lone survivor. I made sure to give each of my boys a shot at being the hero at the end of each story.

The next day, I'd go up to the sixth floor to show them what I wrote. They'd crowd around me in anticipation as I sat on the steps to start reading to them. My little homies loved those stories, quiet and listening intently except for making the occasional comments draped in excitement and fear.

"…the killer then stuck a pencil inside Joe's eye." I read.

"Oh!" Erin whispered.

"Damn, that hurt." Joe giggled.

"That's fucked up." Mikey whispered.

"I don't wanna die like that." Little Jay agreed.

"Read it again." three-year-old Keane would say when I was done, as if I was reading him a bedtime story.

Writing was my way of getting my mind off my father, using my imagination to create some dopeness and not focus on the random thoughts about him that usually came out of nowhere, attacking my brain and tormenting my heart and soul for the fuck of it. Creativity was the antidote. I looked forward to writing. It gave me determination. Joy. It was a challenge, like putting a puzzle together or figuring out a riddle. But better. I was creating something out of nothing, something I could say I invented from scratch, mine all mine. I didn't buy it at the store. I didn't record it off the TV. I didn't borrow it. It was an original work of art.

What I felt in my chest after finishing each of those joints was a feeling I'm not sure I had ever felt before, synonymous with accomplishment. It was the top level of satisfaction. All I know is that shit felt good. After those first few tales of hood horror, I knew I was never gonna put the pen down.

Those stories I had written were fiction just like the movies we used to watch, but at the time, I didn't know that thirty years later I'd have a history of real horrors to write about.

My boy Ant was the real talent, though; he created his own comic books based on scary shit. Had never been to art school, yet his drawing skills were off the fuckin' hook!

But Ant loved that horror shit just a little too much. One day, he made up the game *Friday the 13th*, which was basically *Manhunt* but with actual violence.

With any other game, we usually gathered in a circle, put one foot in, and went through the whole "Eeny-meeny-miny-moe, catch a tiger by the toe" routine. But with *Friday the 13th*, that wasn't needed. While every other kid hated being picked to have to chase everybody around, when it came to playing as the killer Jason, Ant yelled, "I'm it!", every single time we played. Everyone was okay with it at first, but since his gameplay got rougher every time we played, *Friday the 13th* eventually died out.

Ant was a big-boned and strong Italian and Puerto Rican kid that looked eighteen instead of twelve. When playing *Friday the 13th*, the rest of us would only simulate the violence. But not Ant; he'd catch kids, manhandle them, and maliciously dig his clip-needy, jagged, dirty nails into their flesh, fuckin' up arms, necks, shoulders, backs, and ribcages in the process. He also used a small piece of branch as his make-believe knife and jabbed everybody with it way too fuckin' hard. I wouldn't say he was a bully, but Ant really got too deep into that shit. It was obvious

137

he got his kicks from watching peoples' reactions to pain; his face lit up with a perverse expression whenever a kid screamed or complained. Everybody but him returned home from the park with black-and-blues and scrapes and scratches.

The previous summer, in '79, I had gone to see the movie *The Warriors*, and as dope as it was, The Warriors looked like a bunch of bitches compared to the gangs of Washington Heights. I had already seen members of the Uptown Crazy Crew in the area—Chino was supposed to be one of their crazier guys, a skinny, loud Puerto Rican with slanted eyes and a mean limp. But in early June, I saw the Ball Busters marching through my block on the day of the Puerto Rican Day parade. Those brothers looked intimidating as fuck as they proudly held the island's flags over their heads. The Sugarhill Gang's *Rapper's Delight* was playing on a mega-boombox one of them was carrying on his shoulder.

The line from the song that stood out to me the most was the one where Big Bank Hank suggested that if your girlfriend was acting up, then you were better off leaving her behind and instead taking *her friend* to the Holiday Inn. Or any hotel or motel for that matter. *Shit*, where I come from, even a rooftop will do.

But fuck the bullshit; besides the braggadocio being spit all over the song, there were a couple of jewels on there for a shorty like me to learn from. It was probably done subconsciously, but after listening to Big Bank Hank say it so many times throughout the years, from my teens on up I ain't think there was anything wrong with messing with my girlfriends' friends every now and then as long as they never found out. (Thanks to whoever really originated that line, Grandmaster Caz or DJ Hollywood.)

The Playboys was another well-respected gang in the Heights. In '82, when fall came back around and school started again, and Moms bought me a black Playboy jacket with the dark gray, glossy Playboy shoes to match, I thought I was the shit. But it had nothing to do with the gang; it was 'cause that bunny logo was on everything in those days, and I ain't know too many other kids that had it on their clothes. I felt exclusive. Rocking some shit that others ain't have made me feel like I was in my own lane, even at the early age of twelve. But I was humble about it; I wasn't doing any cartwheels or anything like that to get noticed like Erin would have done.

The Playboy jacket had a row of bunny heads across the chest and back, and also circling around each arm at the biceps. Other cats were walking around in Chinese suits and slippers, the shit Bruce Lee had on in his movies. I wasn't with that shit; they had the streets looking like it was Halloween every day of the week.

The Bronx was flooded with the Savage Nomads, Black Spades, and Savage Skulls among other gangs. They were older crews that still rocked denim and leather vests that advertised their gang names on the back. Newer gangs wore beads; necklaces made of two different color beads around their necks identified who they were. I hadn't been there that much except for the few times on foot with C-lo and Ant, by bus to the roller rink Skate Key with my sisters and their friends, and for my mother's three yearly shopping trips for school, winter, and summer clothes at Alexander's department store on Fordham Road, but I remember a lot of the Boogie Down Bronx looking like it was the end of the world.

A couple of years later, I would start hearing about the Manhattan Blood Brothers, Born To Kill, and Fuck The World, followed by the Fresh Kings, Criminal Boys, Wild Creations, Fresh Writers, and countless other Uptown crews another two or three years down the line.

In the early evenings, I used to sit on the poles outside my building and wonder where my father could be. As it got darker and colder and less people passed by, I routinely studied this guy that used to stand on the corner across the street every night. He was doing his shift and I was doing mine. The only difference was that he was earning money, and I was earning knowledge by observing everything around me.

The young hustler, maybe only in his early twenties, was a Puerto Rican dude—chinky-eyed just like Chino and the people he got *his* name from—who usually wore Lee jeans, a hooded sweatshirt, Adidas sneakers, and a fedora hat, a style made famous by rap group Run-DMC a few years later. (A black, crazy-eyed Cuban that resembled Wesley Snipes was his boss. Even over thirty-five years later, as he's approaching sixty, his body is still cut up and sculpted with the ill six-pack.) Every time certain people came up to him, he used a milk crate to climb up and reach behind the awning of the closed Fruit Stand. From there, he'd fetch what looked like a sandwich baggie. Whatever he was digging for in that little plastic bag was too small for me to see, but I know people always exchanged money for it.

I ain't give a fuck about that. I just wanted to rock the same gear as that cat. He was unique in the way that he dressed. I don't remember anybody else in the Heights with that style at the time. They might have been rocking some of the same shit, but he was on that next level as far as the way he combined his shit and sported certain fly shit first, the type of dude that started trends; he had to be from the Bronx or Harlem. This guy was so cool that if he was sporting a pair of suede Pumas on a rainy day, they'd be wrapped entirely in Ziploc wrap to protect them from getting wet. Not only the Pumas, but also the fedora would be tightly wrapped. I was impressed. I had found my style. I wanted to be a b-boy.

There were nights where I didn't go back up to my crib until after that dude retrieved his stash and walked off towards 181st Street about ten o'clock at night. He probably had to catch a bus or the number 1 train back to his own hood. It's like I said before, he was doing his shift and I was doing mine. His nightly departure from the block was my signal that it was time to go home. I'd turn around to walk to the building entrance and there was mom every time sitting on the little balcony on the window, watching me while she smoked her Parliaments. So, I guess it's safe to say that Moms had a shift, too, and just like mine, that shift would gain overtime hours as the years went by.

That year, Boogie's stepfather's drunken antics got crazier. While we played games like *Tag* and *Johnny Ride the Pony* in the sixth-floor hallway, Cheo would come upstairs and chase us out with his big

German Sheppard in one hand and a black nine-millimeter pistol in the other. That's right—an old man with a gat was terrorizing kids ranging from four to eleven years old like he was on a murder spree. That lasted a couple of years.

"Maldito carajitos! Dejen de hacer tanta bulla!" ("Goddamn kids! Stop making so much noise!") Cheo yelled, even though he lived on the second floor and couldn't even hear us from the inside of his apartment.

Some kids ran home while the rest of us hit the streets for a couple of hours before meeting up in the hallway again. The brothers Erin and Keane and my other friend Bighead Benny were the only ones with fathers in their households, but they never told them about Cheo 'cause they ain't wanna be told that they couldn't play in the hallway anymore, so his crazy, drunk ass got away with that bullshit for a long time. I ain't wanna worry Moms so I never told her about him either.

Poisonous Darts

One day, Ant and C-lo decided to test how much heart I had outside the 182nd Street schoolyard; they dared me to throw a stick through some kid's bicycle tires as he rode by.

"Who, Peppermint Patty?" I asked, referring to the freckles on his face and bowl-shaped hairstyle the kid had just like the Charlie Brown character.

Ant and C-lo busted out laughing.

"Oh, shit, he does look like Peppermint Patty!" said a wide-grinned C-lo. "But Peppermint Patty is a girl, though."

"So is he." I sarcastically replied while sizing up the kid. Ant and C-lo laughed some more.

"Go ahead, Gus, don't be scared. That kid is a punk!" Ant pressured.

"I ain't scared. I got this."

I waited for the kid to pass me and threw the stick into the spokes of his back tire. The bike automatically stopped, and he fell off.

"Why did you do that?!"

"Because I felt like it...so what?" I responded, feeling like I could beat the kid in a fight since we were the same size.

"Tioooooo!" ("Uncleeeeee!"), the kid yelled as he ran into the schoolyard, where his uncle was playing basketball with a group of at least fifteen other men. *"Ese muchacho me tumbo de la bicicleta!"* ("That kid knocked me off my bike!")

They all came out to the sidewalk to confront me. I was surrounded. A few of them were the big brothers and cousins of the angry kids I had been in the third and fourth grades with.

"Cual fue? Este Boricuita?" ("Which one was it? This little Puerto Rican?"), his uncle, a thin, five-eight-ish man with a medium afro asked. The afro made him look taller than he was.

The word *"Boricuita"* slid off his tongue like he had the taste of shit in his mouth; he had an obvious disgust in his tone, which also expressed itself clearly with a nasty smirk on his face. I didn't know the value of that deadly combination back then, but now I'm wise enough to recognize what it was; the hatred my classmates had for me was a result of what they had learned from these men that were in their twenties and thirties; they had something against Blacks *and* Puerto Ricans.

In hindsight, it all makes sense now; Ricardo and the other two mad kids from my class had no problem speaking to Boogie and Little Jay; they were both Dominican. But when it came to Mikey, Bighead Benny, and me, there was a dose of hostility whenever *any* words were exchanged.

"*Por qué lo hiciste?*" ("Why did you do it?")

I shrugged my shoulders.

"*Oh, tú no sabes?*" ("Oh, you don't know?"), he sarcastically questioned again and then looked at all his peoples and they all started laughing. "*Pues esto es lo que vamos hacer: yo le voy a aguantar las manos a los dos, y cuando yo cuente a tres y los suerte, se ponen a pelear...okay?*" ("So, this is what we're going to do: I'm going to hold both of you guys' hands, and when I count to three and let go, you start fighting...okay?"), he suggested with a sneaky grin.

"*Si, tío.*" ("Yes, uncle."), the kid replied.

I nodded my head in approval. Being that I had already been in a couple of fights on the block that were either close or I flat-out won, I felt confident about beating his nephew's ass. The kid's uncle cuffed both of my wrists with his left hand and did the same to his nephew with his right. And the countdown began.

"*Uno!*"

I looked over at my boys like, "I got this!"

"*Dos!*"

I looked at my opponent and he had the same anxious look I had. We were both ready to scrap. His uncle jerked our hands up and down with each count.

"*Tres!*"

145

That punk-ass uncle of his only let his nephew's hands go free while he still held my little ten-year-old wrists tight like shackles. The kid swung for my face, but instead hit my chest when I managed to pull my head back, and as soon as his hand touched me, his uncle pushed me down to the ground, making it look like his nephew's punching power did it.

"Gano mi sobrinooo!" ("My nephew wiiins!"), Uncle Bitch-Ass cheered.

He and his buddies then rushed his nephew back into the schoolyard with them to protect him from getting hit back. They all cheered for him and laughed at me and got right back into their basketball game. I got off the floor feeling deceived and embarrassed, mad as hell that my father wasn't around; I just knew he would have fucked that scrawny dude up.

But it wasn't over yet.

My sister Leticia's friend, Marisol, lived across the street and had seen what happened from her window. While it was all going down, she had called Leticia on the phone, and just as I finished brushing myself off, my sister came running into the block.

"Who's the man that pushed you?!" she asked, getting right to the point. Leticia looked like she was ready to kick ass.

"The skinny guy with the afro!"

"They *all* got afros!" Leticia yelled. She was right; that shit was looking like The Jackson Five Times Three in there.

"The one with the red tank top!"

Leticia ran into the schoolyard screaming. "Why'd you put your fuckin' hands on my brother?! Why don't you push *me*, huh, you fuckin' skinny toothpick *motherfucka*?!"

Uncle Bitch-Ass tried to dodge her, but his boys were in his way. Leticia pounced on him without hesitation. She might have hit like a girl, but she was punching and hammering that sucker on his arms, his face, his back, anything she could hit. Even his afro took some lumps. My sister was only fifteen, but she was a beast. He tried to block the attack, but his skinny ass was visibly getting hurt in the process. His friends also tried to stop Leticia, but quickly backed off when she hit them too.

"Don't you ever touch my brother again, motherfucka!"

It felt good to trade places with that punk. When Leticia finally let up on him, the embarrassment stuck on his face was as deep as the hatred it had on it just a few minutes before. I just smirked at him and all his friends. Marisol came running down from her mother's house and led Leticia out of the schoolyard, but I could still hear her cursing up a storm a block away. My sister was one tough bitch, as hardbody and fierce as they come.

As the Rhyme Goes On

It felt like a year had passed, but just a couple of months after my father's disappearance, Moms found a small piece of paper in one of the pants he left behind. It had something written in his handwriting. I don't know what it was, but it led Moms and Leticia to another apartment in our building on the second floor. A Honduran couple only a few years older than Pops answered the door. My mother showed them a picture of my father and asked if they knew him. They did. And they were surprised to find out that just the year before he had lived on the floor above with us, his family. But my mother and sister were even more surprised to hear that he had run off with a much younger woman—the couple's daughter—and married her the day after he left us.

The woman's parents told her about my mother's visit, no doubt, and another few months later, near the end of the school year, Pops thought it was okay to come back around since his big secret was out.

He never got out of his car, though; he just stayed in the safety of his station wagon. I guess he ain't wanna bump into Moms or any of us on the sidewalk or inside the building. But that shit wasn't gonna keep Leticia from getting at him.

One night, *Papi* rolled up on the block, double-parked in front of the building, and waited in the car while his new wife went upstairs to visit her parents.

I bet he never saw it coming.

Leticia barged out of the building with a baseball bat and began smashing the car's headlights.

"You motherfucka, how the fuck could you leave us?!" she screamed, as she ran to the back of the car and also bashed in the rear brake lights. Leticia was furious with tears streaming down her face.

My father pleaded with her to stop and nervously closed his car window. He got the look of the big Rodney Dangerfield eyes, but this time he wasn't mad, he was scared. I didn't think it was funny. I watched it happening from our window balcony with my mother and Cookie. It was surreal; I couldn't believe what I was seeing. When the car lights were all destroyed, she wiped her flushed face—the crying gone but the hurt and hatred still there—and walked back inside the building. Only then did my father get out and examine the damage. He momentarily glanced up at our window and upon seeing us there, I could only describe shame in his eyes before he rushed back into his car. When his wife walked back out of the building, she first looked up at our window—and probably shitted on herself when she saw all of us there

149

staring down at her—before noticing how fucked up the car was. I was lost and too young to catch it, but it was then that the rest of my family realized his wife had been aware of us all along. Me, I initially had that pain of seeing him go, but then I just drifted back into the demolition I had just witnessed, and after seeing Leticia in action for the second time, I knew she was no fuckin' joke.

My father called my mother within a week to try and peace things out. He then picked us all up a few nights later, and while he, my sisters, and my mother sat and talked on some park benches in Spanish Harlem, I played with the radio inside his car.

I swiveled the knob to the right.

-Rock.

Swiveled again.

-Static.

-White men talking about nothing.

-Static.

-Rock.

-Marvin Gaye.

-Static.

-Folk.

-Rock.

-Country.

Sheesh.

Then the swiveling just became a game of racing up and down the dial, just fucking with it, until I stopped around the middle and skidded onto some dope shit. The song had a medium-tempo beat and a simple but funky-ass bassline. After a couple of seconds, a smooth voice started rhyming.

It was Hip Hop.

I was stuck.

I had heard *Rapper's Delight*, and my favorite joint up to that moment, *Adventures of Super Rhymes* ('cause of that slick shit he had done—rapping as Dracula and the rhyming equivalent of the Man of Steel), and they were both catchy songs, but this one was different. He wasn't talking about owning expensive cars and mansions or eating a piece of chicken that tasted like wood like The Sugarhill Gang, or kickin' some cartoonish shit like Jimmy Spicer, but instead he was telling a realistic story, something I could believe happened to him. The rapper's name was Spoonie Gee and the song was called *Spoonin' Rap*. I had heard it before in the streets but never really gave it my full attention.

"Say I was drivin' down the street on a stormy night..."

As he kicked his rhyme about driving around in his car and jumping out to rap to a girl with a fat ass in the hood, I pictured it being somebody in the same streets as me, somebody right there in Harlem. I watched cars as they drove by and wondered.

Maybe that's him in that car right there. Or that one!

Even though I had already lived in New York, Connecticut, and Puerto Rico by the age of ten, the world was still that small to me. But it turned out Spoonie Gee really *was* from Harlem.

151

That night in my father's car, I was mesmerized by the way Spoonie was putting his words together and telling his story. His laid-back flow, the beat, and that spoon-tapping sound throughout the record had me hooked! It was the best music I had ever heard.

Before that, the theme music to my life had been Folk, Soul, Disco, Salsa, and all that old Frank Sinatra and Dean Martin type of shit, with snippets of Rock being played here and there. But now it was a wrap; Hip Hop had officially taken over my world.

Every time I've heard *Spoonin' Rap* for over the last thirty-five years, I'm reminded of that night. I know exactly where I was. Not only because it was a life-changing event for me, but also 'cause of the bullshit that was going on with Pops.

It's some devastating shit to a kid when his father's not in the picture anymore, and there I was, finally having the chance to spend time with mine after almost a year—excited about seeing him—but instead of being out there with him, I was paralyzed in the passenger seat of his car, listening to Spoonie Gee like if the coolest cat on the planet was dropping game on me. His song had an even more powerful impact on me than anything my family was going through and the fact of my pops being or not being around. At that moment, *Spoonin' Rap* was all that mattered.

Hip Hop eventually became my new father. Or at least that big brother I never had—closest thing to that was my boy Eddie, but he ain't even live in the building yet. It would go on to teach me a lot of the things that my own pops should have taught me. Its voices would put me on to important people and incidents I really didn't know shit about. Even though I had seen them on mad portraits being sold all along 125th Street in Harlem, I was basically blind to who Martin Luther King Jr. and Malcom X really were until rappers like Public Enemy, KRS-One, X-Clan, and even The Juice Crew mentioned them and put their images or pieces of their speeches in their songs and videos.

On the album cover of Boogie Down Productions' *By All Means Necessary*, KRS-One peeking out of a window with an Uzi in his hand, recreating the Malcom X picture I had only seen in Harlem before, threw the question in my mind in huge neon letters: Who is this man and why is he holding a rifle and looking out that window as if he's being hunted?

Biz Markie was the first one to make me wonder who the fuck somebody was when he rapped, *"Reagan is the Prez, but I voted for Shirley Chisholm"*; I knew who Ronald Reagan was—the dude they showed getting shot at on Eyewitness News like a thousand times when I came home from school one day—but my mind was hungry about knowing who this Shirley Chisholm was. I wasn't the type to go running to the library for some info, though; I usually learned a little somethin' by building with the older heads and blowing through newspapers front to back. But years later, as the name still rung bells in my head, I did take time to read more about her and the others. Until then, I always thought Biz was saying "Shirley Chizum". You can imagine how hard it was for me to find her while typing that into the Internet.

One time in '95, as I was about to ride a Greyhound bus as the backup of a little Dominican *mami* that was transporting a brick of coke

153

to Ohio, and I needed a book to read for the fifteen-hour trip, I figured *The Autobiography of Malcom X* would be the perfect choice to kill time, and it really was. The point being that even though it had been about five years since Public Enemy's Chuck D had said, *"'cause a Black hand squeezed on Malcom X the man"*, and seven years since the BDP album cover, I still felt I needed to learn more about him; having that knowledge was important to me. I knew what Chuck D was saying, but I still needed to know the whole story leading up to that, and there was no better way than reading it in Malcolm X's own words.

There was a lot more crucial information I learned through Hip Hop before anybody else broke it down to me.

Devastating Tito and the rapper Jalil both warned me about the gossipers and the haters on The Fearless Four's *Problems of the World Today* and Whodini's *Big Mouth*.

Just-Ice dropped science on hoes and some real foreign shit I ain't know about—the shit you could catch from them. On *That Girl Is A Slut*, he said, *"I'll be goddamned, I'm not catching any crabs, or herpes, or them nasty little AIDS going around!"* Kool Moe Dee put his two cents in on that when he had to *Go See the Doctor*, as he rapped about waking up one morning yelling like a motherfucka after finding his joint drippin' and pussin'.

That was some hardcore shit to a fifteen-year-old kid that still hadn't got any ass yet. Thinking about my dick being on fire and some nasty-ass pus dripping out of it was crazy. Not scary, just crazy—some surreal, science-fiction-flick type of shit.

When Kool G Rap said, *"They got a nice, warm welcome for new inmates, razors and shanks and sharp-edged plates, posses will devour, punks with power, after the shower, it's...rush hour!"*, I understood that *Rikers Island* wasn't the place for me. But later on, my hardheaded ass ignored G Rap's advice and eventually wound up in there anyway. That wasn't *his* fault, though; he definitely had let me know what to expect.

Shit, Biz even told me about using a tissue or a Q-tip when *Pickin' Boogers*! That was a lesson in hygiene.

Hip Hop also helped expand my vocabulary. Rappers like T La Rock, LL Cool J, and Kool Keith steadily kept dropping some big-ass words on my head like I was at a spelling bee.

T La Rock spit, *"Commentating, illustrating, description giving, adjective expert"* on *It's Yours.* Those first two bars alone made me feel like I was in some type of big boardroom meeting of high-profile executives right there in my little-ass bedroom.

On LL Cool J's first joint, *I Need A Beat,* he used words like syncopate, elevate, excel, infiltrating, and acute. I knew he was just a teen like me, but this motherfucker sounded like a professor! Those words were dope as fuck to me. I probably had heard them before in the mouths of teachers or characters in TV shows like *The Bionic Man* and *The Incredible Hulk,* but hearing them being spit in rhymes definitely took them off the nerdy list.

Kool Keith killed it better than all of them, though, coming off like an incredibly-deranged master scientist at NASA on the Ultramagnetic MC's *Ego Trippin'.* At the beginning of the second verse, he rapped without rhyming, *"Choosing scientific matter, I prone for evidence, leading melodies obtaining slight positive beams"*. Then a few bars later, he obliterated other rappers with—

> *"Microwave frequencies, directly inorganic,*
> *operating logically, new developments,*
> *separate accumulating ambiguous thoughts,*
> *admitting parts specify particular words,*
> *volunteer agitating ears of parasites,*
> *respond duplicating attempting lyricists,*
> *like a knowledge competition, an ultimate reality,*
> *the General speaker Corporal Kool Keith,*
> *leaving specimens frozen in zero degrees,*
> *by controlling every germ, a spray disinfectant,*
> *with tranquilized brains and stunned competi-tors,*
> *'cause we're ULTRA! magnetic, magnetic*
> *MC's ULTRA! magnetic, magnetic"*

I ain't know what a lot of that shit meant, but you can bet I picked up the dictionary in my crib and sharpened my linguistics only because of what these cats were saying.

Rakim dropped a lot of knowledge and new words on me, too, but if it's one thing about him I remember the most, it's that when I first heard him say what he would do to twenty-one MC's on *Check Out My Melody*, I just knew he was the fuckin' illest.

The realest song to come out after *Spoonin' Rap* was Grandmaster Flash and The Furious Five's *The Message*. Their detailed rhymes gave the whole planet a window into their world, streets that people from different walks of life would never have believed existed if not for the song and video, the same streets I had walked through with C-lo and the fellas on our little exploring missions to nowhere. But back then, I thought everybody knew all about those streets. In my head, the world was much smaller.

Back on the park benches, my father made all the promises deadbeat daddies make—to take care of me and my sisters financially and see us on a regular basis—but that only happened once or twice a year if we were lucky, the part about seeing us; the money part, even less.

As for Spoonie Gee, I still picture him today driving around Harlem, living exactly what he was saying on that song.

Got It Bad Y'all

On December 31st, 1981, a year-and-a-half had passed, but my
family was still trying to get used to not having my father around. We
weren't doing great, but we weren't down in the dumps either. Honestly,
I ain't notice much of a difference in our living conditions. My mother
had gotten us on public assistance and was able to get a part-time job at
her friend's dry cleaners in the hood to hold us down. Even though times
were hard, she still managed to give us a dope-ass Christmas like we
were used to.

People nowadays talk about how they were embarrassed to use food
stamps; how they tried to avoid being seen and waited until the coast
was clear to pull out their funny-money booklets. But I never really
cared 'cause just about everybody else was flashing that colorful
Monopoly money at the *Los Primos* bodega. Besides, most of the kids
making fun of welfare kids were kids on welfare themselves. By my

standards, money was money, only that I couldn't buy toys and movie tickets with the welfare kind.

Anyway, to get our minds off my father, Moms decided it would be a good idea to throw a big New Year's bash at the crib and invite all our relatives from the tri-state area—nothing fancy that she couldn't afford, just good food and music. Everybody from 174th, Brooklyn, New Jersey, and Connecticut was coming. We had never done a celebration of that magnitude while living at apartment 38, so Moms' and my sisters' excitement was on blast-off. They spent the early part of the day cooking, cleaning, and getting our house ready for the party. I was excited that I would be seeing my cousins too, but I had some pre-party shit going on first, an appetizer before the real festivities began.

It was supposed to be one of the happiest memories of our lives, but 'cause of me and my fuckin' stuntman tendencies, it would become a nightmare instead.

Bighead Benny and me had gotten permission to go to the RKO that afternoon to see a triple feature: *Halloween*, *Friday the 13th*, and *Phantasm*. It was a big deal to us 'cause they usually ain't show any triple features there; it was a one-night-only New Year's Eve event. Plus, all three flicks were certified dopeness. We were about to get some popcorn and fake large Coke's and bug out on some mass murder shit. It was bound to be a fun night.

We left the block at about four o'clock and the first movie was scheduled to start in a few minutes, so Bighead Benny and me ran down to the corner of Broadway, passing Pops' old meat market on the way down. I probably thought about him for a half-a-second. That always happened when I saw the place, even after I was grown. It wasn't a meat market anymore; being that it was on the Greek block (the two buildings had nothing but Greek tenants and they did their best to keep it that way for at least a few decades), it made sense that it got turned into a Greek social club. No Niggas Or Spicaroos Allowed. That's how it felt to me every time I saw the small group of white men in front of it.

I kept it movin'. We had two more blocks to go.

As usual, holiday traffic was thick, but it was moving fast. I looked at the Car Wash on the other side of the four lanes in front of me. *I gotta get over there.* It was probably more of a natural reflex than a thought. We were running late so there was only one thing we could do, something we'd already done hundreds of times before, a favorite pastime of all New Yorkers—we had to dodge speeding cars. It was the only way to get to the other side of the street faster. I wasn't trying to miss that opening scene of *Halloween*; the one where little crazy Michael Myers is in his clown costume stabbing up his sister. So what I'd already seen it like five times? That shit was dope.

Bighead Benny ran out first. I timed the oncoming traffic and jumped out onto the four lanes of Broadway right after him. I glided between two speeding cars, stopped after the first northbound lane, let another car pass in front of me, and then sprinted to the yellow line in the middle of the street; I was halfway there. Bighead Benny had already made it all the way across with no problem. I saw that the traffic light was yellow, about to turn red, let the last car going southbound pass me, ran out, and BOOM…I was overcome by total confusion for like three seconds. Everything was moving at a crazy high speed. I saw a flash before my eyes. It wasn't my life flashing in front of me like people be saying after having near-death experiences. Something was flying by me at what seemed like the speed of light. Or was *I* the one flying? It was a blur; a blur of things I couldn't decipher at that moment, but later understood that they were buildings, light posts, street signs, a gas station, cars, tires, and lastly, the hard concrete of the street; in that exact order.

I blacked out.

It couldn't have been but a few seconds. I slowly opened my eyes as my head felt like it was spinning to a slow halt. There was a huge commotion, and people were yelling and standing over me. I heard car doors slamming shut as more people were running over to surround me. I now realized I was lying on my right side on the cold asphalt of Broadway. Although some people were telling me not to move, I couldn't move even if I tried. I ain't feel any pain; I just couldn't move. Maybe I was in shock. A man took off his jacket and gently placed it under my head to support it. The Cuban owner of the only bodega nearby came to see what all the fuss was about and then took off running back to his store to call 911. (I thanked him more than twenty years later when I stopped by his bodega to cop a philly blunt and saw the now gray-haired good samaritan still working behind the counter.)

Bighead Benny shoved his way through the crowd to get a glimpse of who got hit by the car. His jaw dropped when he saw me laid out on the ground like a worn-out welcome mat.

"Gus!"

Bighead Benny was already the color of milk, but at that precise moment that motherfucker turned pale.

"Go get my mom." I managed to force the words out in a little more than a whisper.

Bighead Benny just stood there frozen and speechless for a few more seconds before pushing his way back out of the growing crowd and running up the steep hill that led to our block. Everyone around me was still yelling, some concerned about me, and others pissed off about the traffic jam I had caused. Some were saying that I was thrown the length of a block. I believed it after noticing that I was now in front of the Social Security building on 182nd Street. I stopped looking at them and stared straight ahead. My heart sunk when I spotted my brand-new white-on-burgundy suede Pumas—now stained in oil and grease and whatever else they picked up off of Broadway—scattered beneath some cars. *Not my Pumas. I just got those on Christmas.*

The accident scene was three blocks from my building, but Bighead Benny made it back with my mother and sisters mad fast, just as some paramedics were jumping out of an ambulance. I still wasn't sure if I was even injured at all. But that was answered as soon as my family laid eyes on me. My mother was strong. She remained as calm as possible in order to not scare me any further. But I could read her face, though;

she was both sad and terrified. My sisters Aggie and Cookie cried softly. But Leticia flipped the fuck out. After someone pointed out the reckless driver of the car that hit me, she got enraged, banged her fists on the hood of a car that stood between them, and tried to attack him. The poor man ran circles around the car until a couple of cops restrained Leticia.

My right arm was twisted all the way around at the shoulder and was kind of helping the jacket support my head. After one paramedic started cutting off my black corduroys and got to my knee, he accidently blurted out, "Oh, shit." Something took him by surprise. I couldn't look down at my legs, but the spectators' reactions around me let me know it was nothing pretty.

"What is it?" I asked. "Is it big?"

He hesitated. "It's a little big." Dude was disgusted.

I had a gash on my left leg that started from under the front of my knee and circled around, ending behind it with an upwards turn. The inner part of my knee had a gaping hole; a huge chunk of flesh had been ripped right off of me. Basically, my leg was almost chopped-off at the knee. Three bones around the knee area had been fractured. My right shoulder and ankle had also been fractured, and the ankle had an inch-long slice over the bone that sticks out on one side.

I was all fucked up and still was more upset about my fucked-up Pumas and not making it to the triple feature at the RKO than I was about my own condition.

It was a miracle how I didn't have any head injuries. I had been thrown over a murderous amount of cars and then bounced and slid on the ground beside them in the midst of New Year's traffic and ain't have one scratch or bruise on my head or face.

At the hospital, I went into surgery right away. When I woke up next, I was in a dark, quiet room with a group of cousins, aunts, uncles, and of course, my mother and sisters surrounding me. A small lamp next to my bed lit the room only bright enough so that I could barely see them. They looked like they were glowing. I didn't know what to think. I was numb. I could lie to you and say I felt good to be alive, but I never even thought about that. While they all stared at me and I stared back, I was calm, without feeling. Numb. I was definitely in shock. I felt like I was in the Twilight Zone. Maybe it was the drugs they had me on. It took a few minutes for me to register and remember why I was there. It was then that I realized my family was standing around me looking like they were holding a vigil for me. It was a good feeling to have them all there for me, but I also felt bad knowing that I had messed up our first big party since coming back to New York. Some of those cousins and uncles were probably mad as fuck that I had messed up their New Year's. It was past midnight.

"Happy New Year."

I lasted three weeks in Columbia-Presbyterian Hospital, my first time back since birth. But it's not like I was happy to be there; I was all fucked up. All my friends from the block visited but I hardly saw them; for the most part, I was left alone in my motionless state 'cause they were more interested in playing at the hospital game room on another floor. My sisters came by every day to help Moms take care of me, rotating shifts and all that.

I was a damn mummy. One arm and one leg-and-a-half were all in casts. My left arm only had limited movement since an I.V. was injected into it. I needed help eating, washing up, pissing and wiping my ass, but I only let the nurses do most of that.

Aggie would bring me all kinds of comic books—Marvel, DC, and some other shit—every other day, but I was always thirsty for more 'cause I ain't have a television in my room; TVs weren't allowed in that section of the hospital so that the other patients could rest and recuperate quietly. But the silence never lasted long in there anyway, so it wouldn't really have mattered. There were five other kids in my room, some in worse conditions than I was, so whether it was the injured or their loved ones, someone was always crying, whimpering, moaning, or screaming in agony and pain. This one smaller kid, for whatever reason, a tube had to be inserted into his dick every day. There was also a girl that had been hit by a car like me. The accident left her so bad that she could hardly speak, only scream her lungs out as if she was being tortured. The curtain around her bed was closed around the clock. I heard she had more broken limbs and stitches than a rag doll. The slightest movement, getting washed up, and the constant prodding of doctors probably felt to her like she was being skinned alive. Their suffering was way worse than mines; I was just given several injections with long-ass needles on a daily.

My father only showed up to see me once. I hadn't seen him since the Spoonie Gee episode. Even though I was by myself when he came by, Pops looked uncomfortable the whole time he was there. He hardly spoke. It was like he didn't know what to say to me. Maybe he was in shock after seeing me all fucked up like that. Maybe he was having regrets of not being there to stop it from happening. (Pops would have never let me go to the theatre with my friends on New Year's Eve; he was too strict for that. Holidays were hardcore family days, "there's no 'I' in team" type of shit. All that running around the city with my homeboys ain't fully start until after he was gone.) Maybe he just didn't know how to be a father anymore. Maybe all the responsibility that comes with that had been lifted off his shoulders since the day he left us, and he had erased Leticia, Cookie, and me from his mind to a certain extent. Why not, from what I could tell he had done the same thing with his first daughter? Maybe he just didn't have the skills anymore or just never had them to begin with.

Pops left after only twenty minutes with me. His excuse for having to leave his could've-been-dead son after only twenty minutes? "I couldn't find any parking. My wife is alone downstairs in my double-parked car." It really had nothing to do with the car. Back in those days you could be double-parked all year-round if you wanted to and the cops wouldn't say shit.

Moms used to say my doctor looked like Jesus. White Jesus, from the portraits. He did—white Jesus straight out of Super Cuts. Young, clean-cut, soft-spoken, and tall with the kindest demeanor ever, Moms said his hands had to have been blessed for him to put me back together like he did. I was grateful.

Dr. Jesus was a thinker, in deep concentration every time he came to see me. Through his small, wire-rimmed glasses, his eyes were always focused on my injuries and his fingers rubbing the chin of his close-cropped beard as he spoke to Moms about my condition and future prognosis. Dude was serious about his art.

After surgery, they had cut a hole in my cast and attached this weird-shaped plastic thing to catch all the blood dripping from the severed part of my knee. I don't know what the fuck it's called but it looked like a bong. The day it had to be taken off, Jesus didn't come. Another fortysomething-ish, black glasses-wearing, madman doctor, erratic and sweaty with messy shoulder-length hair, brutally wrestled it off my leg. He drilled through the cast with an electric device that looked like a pizza cutter while retardedly pushing and pulling on the blood-spattered bong thing. That shit hurt worse than when I got hit by the fuckin' car. After being discharged from the hospital, I never wanted to go back.

I was in a wheelchair for the next three months. I had to go through a routine of Moms cleaning the scarred area, especially the open wound, three times a day. It hurt like hell when she did this; the gauze would always be stuck on me, similar to a Band-Aid on skin, but instead it was attached to raw pink and red flesh. It always took a long while to pull it off as she slowly poured hydrogen peroxide over the injury to loosen it.

It was slow torture watching thin strands of my own flesh stretch out like a rubber band before finally letting go of the blood-soaked gauze.

Being in a wheelchair was kinda fun, though, rolling through my crib like I was on a big-ass tricycle. Little Jay had his roller skates. Joe had his skateboard. I had my wheelchair.

When my mother later started babysitting Little Jay and his older sister Jahaira after school, I sometimes terrorized them. In between gauze changes, Moms would let the monster hole in my leg get some fresh air. So, to kill time, I used to chase them around the house on my wheels at full speed with my wound—a combination of blood, pus, and raw meat—out in the open. Their running and terrified reactions were mad funny. But out on the streets it wasn't fun at all, everybody on their own two feet and me in handicap status.

Soon my mother was able to get a tutor to come to our house on Mondays, Wednesdays, and Fridays—an old, chunky white lady with her frizzy, reddish hair in a bun. Her skin always looked greasy and she stank like kitty litter. When my arm was healed, and I was well enough to roll myself around, I was left at home alone at times while Moms went downtown to work cleaning rich people's homes. You could say this is when I first started cutting classes. At least once or twice a week, when my teacher knocked on our front door, I changed my voice into a deeper tone and told her, "Gus isn't home." After a few times of trying to get me to open the door, she'd finally give up and leave. She was a nice lady and a real good teacher; it was just that I wasn't trying to hang out with her and that nasty stench for four hours a day when I could be doing better things like watching TV.

Shit, I must've been a real crazy little kid if I really thought I was fooling her with my fake adult impersonation. What made me think she wasn't gonna tell Moms that I turned her away? It was like I just didn't give a fuck and was telling her "Get the fuck outta here!" I had to know she was gonna tell Moms. But I probably didn't give a fuck about anything in those days; I was confined to a wheelchair and couldn't run around with my friends like I used to. The wheelchair was almost as bad as a jail cell, like being behind bars right on the street. I was free but incarcerated. While they did all the shit kids did, all I could do was watch.

April and May were spent on crutches, and after the last five months of painful fuckin' therapy—therapists pushing my leg back, bringing my knee to my chin, pulling it back out, me taking the slow-motion steps for learning how to walk again, my body collapsing over my reconstructed knee and ankle—I was ready to go back to school just in time for graduation. My doctors wanted me to use a walking cane until my leg was in tip-top shape again.

"Nah, I ain't trying to look like no old man."

The funny thing is that shortly after that I started seeing more and more teens with those old man walking canes. Canes became b-boy accessories that were supposed to make you look cool, but of course, also came in handy as weapons. I made a huge mistake, though; not wanting to use one for the short time it would take to build up my leg's

169

strength left me with a lifetime permanent limp. But I wasn't mad about it, because while other knuckleheads took years to practice *their* ditty-bop, mine was official.

Beware

Spring 1982. Apartment 38.

The loud sound of a massive amount of glass shattering and Cookie screaming like she's just seen the boogeyman, wakes me the fuck up. Startled out of my sleep, I immediately climb out of my bed and onto my wheelchair mad quick as if I've practiced that shit a thousand times, and then roll out of my room like a wobbly, graffiti-stained subway train to see what the fuck is going on, except the graffiti is left behind in my dreams.

Moms and Leticia run into the living room and I roll in right behind them. It's past midnight and someone's just torpedoed a glass jar through our living room window, managing to scare the shit of my family. Cookie had fallen asleep on the couch earlier while watching TV, but now she's bawling uncontrollably; she's squeezed herself on the floor between the couch and the TV to duck for cover from any other shit that might come through the window. It's the scariest thing to happen to her since moving back to New York. Not in the streets. Not in the subway. Right there in our own home. It's the first but won't be the last. After those mostly quiet years we had spent in the towns of Connecticut and Puerto Rico, we definitely aren't prepared for the craziness that's about to unravel around us throughout the rest of the 80's.

Pops is about his paper, a top-of-the-line hustler
but his mental says "fuck ya" when it comes to family structure
A master of abandonment, in his quest for lavishness
every fuck-up is an accident, he's a fuckin' embarrassment

Poppa Large

That summer, I was almost as good as new but hardly spent any time on the block. Instead, I traveled to Florida three times. The first was by plane when a group of eight family members and one friend hit up Orlando for a two-week vacation. We went to Disney World, Sea World, Wet 'n Wild, and The Wax Museum. Back up north I still hadn't been to anything except old-ass, squeaky Coney Island. Just getting there was torture. You had to ride a couple of trains all the way to Brooklyn for two hours without any AC, trains infested with some of the worst crazies and junkies the City of New York had to offer. Places like Great Adventure and Action Park in New Jersey were urban legends to me, nothing but commercials of happy white people having fun.

Orlando had a couple of arcades the size of city blocks, a huge difference from Manhattan's Playland—a small, crowded Times Square arcade that was full of thugs and was more like the bullpens of Rikers

Island and Central Booking. I'd be shocked if there weren't shanks, knives and guns in there seven days a week.

A few days after getting back, my mother agreed on letting my father take Leticia and me to Miami for another two weeks. I hadn't seen him again since that one time at the hospital.

Pops drove us down in a cargo van. It was half-full of boxes with products for his new business endeavor of selling cosmetics. The van didn't have any back seats, so I had to sit and sleep on the hard iron flooring for most of the thirty-hour trip. Boy, was that shit uncomfortable. Unless I had to take a shit, Pops only stopped so he and Leticia could use the restrooms at the fast food joints and rest stops along I-95. He made me piss by the van's side doors while we sped down the highway. It was sort of like surfing; I was off-balance and spraying everything near those doors. Pops said it would leak out through the doorstep at the bottom but not all of it did. We had to tolerate that lingering smell of urine for hours. Not that it was anything new, certain spots in my building and the schoolyard smelled like that all the time.

Miami reminded me of Puerto Rico; palm trees, beaches, and scorching heat. I liked it a lot. We stayed at an apartment complex that had a tennis court and two pools. Pops had us walking around wearing headbands and shit like we were actual tennis players. Any pictures he took of us had to be while we were in action, either walking or running, no standing still and smiling at the camera. Some premeditated shit; a front. He wanted us to look like we were having fun doing the things we really weren't doing. I was happy for just being able to chill with him. I didn't need to run, swing a tennis racquet, or nothing; I was with my father.

I remember going with Pops to see his sister, *Titi Che-Che*. She looked old enough to be his mother and lived in a nice little home with her even more ancient husband. This was where I first ran into a channel called MTV. It was nothing but music videos. There were only white boys and white girls singing in them, but it was still dope. I sat there watching it, checking out their lifestyles through *Titi Che-Che's* little color TV screen for a few hours.

I had never seen a music video before. The scenery in most of them was just like Miami and what I thought all of California looked like. If you went by the video, they lived good in those places. But I knew it was bullshit. I saw a lot of the same shit in Miami that I had seen in New York; homelessness, dirty streets, rundown homes, and thugs; it was basically a tropical New York.

Pops took us a few times to a cosmetic shop he had opened at a strip mall. One day while he was setting up his merchandise, a Cuban woman wearing a blonde wig and dark shades walked in and scoped the place out. My father whispered to me that it was Mirta de Perales, an entrepreneur in the cosmetics industry. I recognized her; she appeared nightly on television screens in every Latino household that was hooked on *novelas*, hawking her products throughout commercial breaks. I used to get annoyed by the sound of her voice, nasally like if she had bags of coke stuffed up her nostrils and snobbish like if she thought she was the shit.

When she walked out of his store, my father said she was checking to see who her competition was, that it was a good sign. He was positive his new business wouldn't fail like the others. Things were looking good for him; he told me he also had another shop being run by his wife in California. I don't really know if that was true, but as a boy I believed anything my father told me.

By mid-July, we went back home for a few days, and then I returned to Miami with Pops and my other sister Cookie. Leticia stayed behind. She had been throwing up a lot in Miami. I thought she was just sick. But on the low, she was sixteen and pregnant.

Even though my father had taken us down there with the good gesture of having us spend time with him, we hardly saw him at all for the next four weeks; he left us in the home of some friends while he supposedly drove back up north to get more merchandise. It was cool, though. We stayed in a big house that had a pool with a slide and even a sauna in the back of it.

On our way back to New York the second time, my father brought along some new acquaintances he had made; two loud and obnoxious Cuban ladies. I thought they were crazy. That ride was mad hectic since all they did was drink beer, talk shit, and laugh the whole way. Instead of making it a worthwhile road trip with his kids—since he had no intention of seeing us again for a long-ass time—he again concentrated his attention on friends, even though this time they were really strangers.

Thinking back on it now, I realize those women were old school hoodrats, classic middle-aged bitches that were still trying to be young, wearing tight colorful clothes with their kangaroo pouches bulging out at the waist and about a pound of make up on their faces.

Yap-yap-yap.

Thirty hours of that.

The only break from it was when Pops parked and took short naps on the side of the road. The two ladies would use that time to get out and stretch their legs while still running their mouths outside. But at least then their talking was muffled.

Who knows, maybe they were coked up.

Me knowing my father, I'm sure he fronted on how he was a wealthy businessman and probably brought them to see the big city with plans of having sex with one, if not both of them. Years later, he told me they both died of AIDS. I guess Pops ain't get to smash any of them 'cause he's still alive and kicking today.

With all the trips he made up and down I-95, and Miami being Cocaine Central at the time, I sometimes wonder if cosmetics-related merchandise was all he was transporting. My father was a live dude who'd hustle anything, so I wouldn't put it past him to have dabbled in the coke trade at some time or another; there was just too much money to be made.

Shit, my father once told me he even rocked a pair of shades and played the blind man role when he first arrived in Miami penniless. And after establishing himself in New York in those early days, he still occasionally did that scam when his funds were low, and he wanted to go out drinking with his friends.

Welcome to the Terrordome

In elementary school, most of the kids I knew were shook about graduating from PS 132 and moving on to the infamous Junior High School 143 two blocks down; it's rep was almost as bad as that of the South Bronx; kids getting jumped, stick-ups at gunpoint in the bathrooms, apache lines, gang wars—it had it all! As far back as the fifth grade, kids were talking about how they ain't wanna go there, that they'd rather take buses and trains to some other joints across Manhattan. I didn't feel that way. I wanted to go see all the craziness with my own eyes.

So, on my twelfth birthday, the first day of school, I threw on my new gray Le Tigre shirt, black Lee jeans, and white-on-gray suede Pumas, and went to see if I could survive in that hellhole.

I walked into my Homeroom class and it was a madhouse—everybody yelling over each other, blackboard erasers flying across the room, chairs and desks screeching over tiled floors after being knocked out of place; the room was a mess. I didn't see any of my old classmates and figured they must have been sent to safer schools outside the neighborhood. There was this one kid with big bulging eyes and a fucked-up beard growing that looked like he belonged in the tenth grade. He was out of control.

"Class, please settle down." a soft-spoken white lady said.

"Shut the fuck up!" the bug-eyed Puerto Rican man-boy from the Bronx yelled at her over everybody else's noise.

"I know you are all excited, it being the first day of—"

"Shut the fuck up!" he repeated.

I was in shock.

"—school, but I need to take attendance." Everyone got quiet and the red-haired woman continued, "My name is Mrs. Adams and I will be your—"

"Shut the fuck up, bitch!" he laughed, and moved around the classroom as he pleased. It was all a game to him.

"—Homeroom teacher. Jose, can you please—"

"No, bitch!"

"—go back to your seat and stop cursing at me?" Mrs. Adams pleaded, her face finally showing a trace of irritation. She obviously knew that teenage psycho well; he was a veteran at One-forty-three.

"Just suspend me already. I wanna go smoke some weed!"

"But it's the first day of school. You just got—"

"I don't give a fuck! Send me home!"

"—here."

"Fuck it!"

Mrs. Adams then calmly took attendance and ignored Jose while he kept fucking with her. That first day, he only attended a few classes. He was high by lunchtime. After two weeks of coming to school on and off, Jose never came back.

Jose's wild behavior was the perfect introduction for what I would experience over the next three years. Before the first week was done, I saw two other holdovers extorting kids right outside the school's main office while the hallways were crowded with students. P-Nut and Pasqualito weren't roughing anybody up, but their body language was menacing.

"Yo, shorty, let me get a quarter?" Pasqualito asked with a threatening glare, him and P-Nut all in the kids' faces.

Those poor kids scrambled into their pockets fast and gave up more than just quarters; they gave up their hearts. Pretty soon, kids started to turn around at the sight of those two and taking longer routes to their classes.

By 1987, that kid Pasqualito went on to become one of the most feared enforcers in the Lenny Boys, a drug gang that was so out of control the media renamed them the Wild Cowboys in the early nineties. He's currently serving 116 years in prison. As for squat and pudgy, pug-faced P-Nut, he didn't grow any taller or bolder, so his tough guy days ended right there at junior high.

One of the first kids I got cool with in my class went by the graffiti name Dag, a short-as-I-was (5'3?), heavy-handed dude with crazy fast reflexes. Another one was Dixon. He was slightly taller than us, but they were both stocky, muscular kids compared to me; I still looked like I was ten. All my new homies turned out to be from the 170's. Kaleem, a crazy Pakistani-American gun collector from around my block, was also in my class.

The most well-known teachers at One-forty-three were Mr. Ehrlich and Mr. Lehrberger. I only had them as substitutes.

Mr. Ehrlich was known for patrolling the hallways and whacking misbehaving and class-cutting kids on the thigh with his blackboard pointer. Mr. Lehrberger's fame came from his fluent use of bad words. All kinds of "fucks", "shits", and "motherfuckers" came out of his mouth daily. Sex jokes were common in his class. Between periods, he'd come out and watch the girls walk the hallways, boldly looking at their bodies like he was on a street corner and sexually harassing them all day long.

"I like your jeans." Mr. Lehrberger would say as twelve-, thirteen-, and fourteen-year-olds passed by his classroom. They just blushed as he continued, "Nice bump. Mind if I ride?"

He was usually dirtier than that.

"You have beautiful lips. Are they the same on the bottom?" he'd ask with a sly smile.

But sometimes he couldn't help himself and went all out as if he had really forgotten where the fuck he was at and that it was kids he was talking to.

"Those pants are so tight, I can see the outline of your *choh-cha*!" he delightedly blurted out through his gap-toothed smile.

It was amazing the shit he got away with all those years. But Mr. Lehrberger finally got busted and came out on the news in 1990; he had been arrested after repeatedly taking a thirteen-year-old student to the school basement to sexually abuse her. That punk-ass pedophile only received one to three years in prison.

Lunch was where everybody would unwind. On Mondays, all the boys would talk about what happened over the weekend on the WWF with Jimmy "Superfly" Snuka and The Iron Sheik and all the other wrestlers, besides chopping it up about other miscellaneous shit. The girls, I don't know what the fuck they were talking about, but every single school day, they all had small paper bags full of candy, and the boys all asked for some like it was pussy. "Let me get some, baby. C'mon, you ain't gimme none since yesterday!" Shit, the girls were like drug dealers and the boys were their loyal fiends, always begging for another piece of Fishes, Mary Jane, Blow Pops, Bubble Yum, Jolly Ranchers and more shit. All those sweets had the boys sweating some of the girls more for their merchandise than their looks. Cherry Now & Laters were Crack before Crack even hit the street!

A lot of funny shit went down in the cafeteria. I recall one time some of the fellas participated in spitting loogies up to the ceiling to see how long they'd stay up there. Every few weeks, we'd remember to look up and check on a thick one that stuck, and this one boy's nasty green mucus was hanging tough like a motherfuckin' icicle all the way until the schoolyear ended.

For a few weeks in my second year there, I remember they let kids get on the microphone for beatbox battles, but one of the occasional food fights eventually killed that off. Beatboxing was the new craze and the whole lunchroom would go wild whether you were dope or you were wack. Some students just got up there to be clowns. There was this one spaghetti-thin Puerto Rican kid that was off the hook, though, doing everything Doug E. Fresh could do, and whenever he got on the mic it was pandemonium. He had on his Le Tigre, his Lee's, and his Adidas like all the other b-boys and wannabes, but he was different; he was a quiet kid who never talked to anybody, kept to himself, and had weird glasses that made his eyes look too big for his face, always reading something—book or comic book (If I could'a thought of a good rap name for him back then, it would'a been Bookworm Supreme). But after that initial look of fear as he slowly walked up to the microphone and then stared out at his audience, he'd tear that shit up like he'd been doing it since birth. When he was done, and everybody was still clapping and screaming and banging their fists on the lunch tables, he'd quietly walk back to his seat and sit down to resume his reading like, "I ain't do it".

Two or three classes had Gym at the same time. That's where I had first seen Razo, the skinny, smiling gang leader of the Crazy Bombers, whose hands extended so wide that one of them alone wrapped itself around a dodge ball almost like it was a baseball. You had to hope to be on his team because when Razo threw the ball, nine times out of ten it painfully knocked you down and left you with welts. When it missed, it crashed into the gym walls with a sonic BOOM! Only Dag was able to stuff Razo's attacks.

Razo was a wiry dude, crazy nice with his hands and a pro at body-slamming people. He could slam you to the floor over and over as if it was nothing. Didn't matter your size or how much you weighed; he hardly broke a sweat and slammed you with the ease of folding some pants. But don't let that gang leader shit fool you; Razo was one of the friendliest people I ever met. Most of the time, he would rather try to talk things out and only fought you if you insisted; after kicking your ass, he'd help you up and show you love.

"See, my man, I didn't wanna do that to you." Razo would ask with a genuine concern, "Are you alright? We good?"

Even into his thirties, long after his crew was nonexistent, I still saw Razo helping the new breed of up-and-coming menaces that tried to fuck with him up off the floor.

"C'mon, kid, let me give you a hug." Razo smiled.

186

Sucker MC's

Back on the block, kids were trying their hand at breakdancing just like every other kid in the city. We put a lot of time into the hardwood floors of our living rooms and the marble-like floors of our building hallways, trying to perfect our moves.

The Bus Terminal had the smoothest floor, though; the maintenance people must have been buffing and waxing it on a daily; so spacious that it was like an arena for breakdancers. I felt like a pro on that shiny linoleum; faster, more experienced, like I could hang with them dudes in Rock Steady. We usually hit it up past eight o'clock at night when there was hardly anybody there.

As soon as it got dark, we also used to go outside the electronics store Savemart, and to Woolworth's, both on 181st Street, to get discarded cardboard boxes, big ones that once held refrigerators and washing machines, so that we could bring them back to the block, throw them on the sidewalk and do our thing.

My moves were basic; footwork, backspin, footwork, maybe try a hand glide or windmill, some more footwork, backspin, then freeze— holding my nuts and looking at you like *You trash*. I was obsessed with learning atomic flairs but couldn't get past one. I mean, I was pretty good but limited 'cause of my knee injury.

Little Jay wasn't really into it, but he mastered this one move nobody else could do. While doing headspins, he'd stop midway through without using his hands, stay upside-down on his head for a few seconds, and then swivel his legs to continue spinning.

Around this time a few other teenagers moved into my building, amongst them that cool motherfucker Eddie and a hyper cat known to his classmates at JHS 143 as *Cantinflas*—at the time his mustache was only growing over the ends of his mouth, just like the Mexican superstar of the same name had it. But on our block, we called him by his graffiti tag, Fic, or just *Pachuquito*.

Pachuquito was the kind of thin that's deceiving with sharp muscle cuts in his arms—skinny like a motherfucker but really an exceptionally powerful and explosive kid. When he approached you to slap your hand five, you had to brace for impact. He didn't obliterate your hand on purpose; that's just the way he was built.

And he was incredibly fast, too.

One day we were hanging out at the chicken spot on our block and *Pachuquito* ran out to the *Mambi* restaurant across the street in the midst

188

of a wild rainstorm, one of them shits where day turns to night in a matter of minutes. Back and forth it was like the length of a block and a half, but he made it back in like eight seconds flat—and only had a few drops of rain visible on his shirt; that kid was so fast that he could dodge hard rain!

Eddie was a master at dancing all kinds of music. And he dressed the part, too. His pop-locking and breakdancing skills were a couple of notches above ours. Punk Rock, Hip Hop, Salsa, Merengue, Freestyle, Reggae, and New Wave, Eddie displayed a different style day after day. He might come out of the building one day dressed like Robert Downey Jr.'s character in *Back To School* with the little hat and shades and everything, and the next day stroll out like he was in *Beat Street*, but whatever it was, Eddie did that shit flawlessly, adding his own dope twist to it. He even rocked those Bruce Lee outfits. But Eddie wasn't fronting; he really knew some of those karate moves. There was nothing he couldn't do. My man Eddie was like a big brother; that dude that put others onto a lot of things, loved by everyone in the hood.

"Yo, guys," Eddie said to me and Mikey when he found us chilling in front of the building one afternoon, "come to my house, I wanna show you this crazy movie."

Me and Mikey followed Eddie up to his family's apartment on the fourth floor. Eddie pushed a tape into the VCR in his room.

"What's the name of the movie?"

"*Caligula.*"

"What's that about?"

189

"Just watch, you ain't never seen nothing this crazy."

The movie was about a crazy emperor. In one scene, he took the virginity of another man's new bride right in front of him and then stuck his fist into the husband's ass so that he wouldn't feel left out. Besides that, it was basically a porno flick full of orgies.

My boy Mikey's eyes were teary 'cause he tried to keep himself from blinking; he didn't wanna miss a second of the action, repeatedly going between expressions of his jaw dropping to the floor and that uncontrollable giggle he was known for. As for me, I kept my composure as I watched the movie, but my little hardrock shorty wanted to bust through my jeans and see what the fuck was going on. Eddie was right; I had never seen something so crazy. As a matter of fact, I had never seen a porno before.

Eddie was the fuckin' man.

A few months later, Eddie brought us upstairs again, anxious to let us hear a song by the new rap group Run-DMC. Until that day, all I knew was that they had a joint called "It's Like That" that was getting mad play on the streets.

After taking us into his living room, Eddie popped a cassette into his tape deck and raised the volume. We waited.

Eddie had a monster sound system that I admired each time I saw it as if it was the first time. His speakers were over five feet tall. He had one in each corner of the room.

After about five seconds of that humming sound that an empty tape makes, the song Sucker MC's came booming out the speakers like King

Kong was banging out the beats and Godzilla was spitting hot lava in my face. It changed my life forever. It was like nothing I had ever heard before. Songs by the Fearless Four, Spoonie G, and Grandmaster Flash and the Furious Five were always being played in the streets and were pure dope, but *Sucker MC's* was on a whole 'nother level. It was the blueprint of boom bap. It crushed everything. Eddie, Mikey, and I stood in the same spot listening to it intently over and over. Eddie must have rewinded it ten times at least. He just smiled at us and bobbed his head with that look of *this is that next shit, fellas!*

Eddie was the fuckin' man.

If Spoonie G, Melle Mell, and all four of the Fearless Four—Devastating Tito, Great Peso, Mike C, and DLB—made me want to rap, *Sucker MC's* was the song that made me *need* to rap. I'm not sure which one made me pick up a pen to write rhymes for the first time, but I do know Run-DMC established my rap addiction; writing every day was a hobby from that point on.

But the sight of deejays spinning records and scratching them to make a brand-new kind of instrument and sound, and my desire to learn how to do that—was even stronger. So, I begged my mother to buy me some equipment.

Over the next few months, Moms got me two turntables and a mixer, one piece at a time. But even when all I had was just one turntable, I was practicing scratching on it like that was my job. I didn't have the money or space for speakers like Eddie's, so I was satisfied with just hooking my stuff up to the double-cassette boombox Moms had bought me down on Delancey Street the year before. (Delancey was Boombox City; it had stores lined up from one corner to another full of all types of small to gigantic, unique and colorful block-shaking boomboxes from top to bottom.)

At first, my boys Boogie and Julio were just starting to get their own equipment too, so we basically put our pieces together and practiced at each other's homes until all of our systems were complete. While I was all about mixing and scratching Hip Hop, Boogie was more into blending R&B songs. That would cause an unexpected beef and blood to be spilled between us later on.

Underground

1983 was a monumental year for me: I had finally gotten all my DJ equipment; my first niece was born; my father was around, kind of; I was running the streets a lot more than before with all the new friends I made at One-forty-three; the streets were liver than ever; I officially became addicted to Hip Hop on a crackhead level, spending Friday and Saturday nights recording all the new shit from the radio mixes on KTU, Kiss, and BLS, dreading midnight 'cause that's when Smokey Robinson's *Quiet Storm* came on to let me know *Mr. Magic's Rap Attack* was over and it was slow jam time, although those joints created a whole different kind of fiend in me with their laid-back grooves and basslines.

Memorex and TDK tapes cluttered my room. I'd be sitting there staring at the radio with my finger pressed down on the pause button, waiting to let it go as soon as I heard anything new come out the speakers. If BLS was playing a song I had already heard, I'd rotate the big, lazy radio dial fifteen times to the left as fast as possible to see if I could catch something new on Kiss; this back-and-forth shit went on for all three hours of the competing mixes; I didn't wanna miss out on anything.

But the streets were calling. So, a lot of times I'd leave a 120-minute cassette recording everything on just one station so that I could go hang out. I timed myself and came back in time an hour later to flip it to the other side. At the end of the night, no matter what time I came home to sleep, I first sifted through whatever I had recorded, fast-forwarding like crazy to find all the new shit.

Hip Hop was sonic crack. My main suppliers throughout the eighties were Red Alert, Chuck Chillout, Mr. Magic & Marley Marl, and the Latin Rascals. Then you had those cats that served you on the late night or during the week when everybody else was off the air, cats like DNA & Hank Love, Lyvio G & P-Fine, and The Awesome Two. The quality of the stations they broadcasted from wasn't crisp and clear, but the product was still banging.

In a way, the underground radio shows felt more personal; since at that time of night the streets and the inside of my crib were so damn quiet, except for the occasional crackhead outburst, in my mind it was like if the world was asleep and it was just me and these radio dudes getting high together on beats and rhymes. The scratchy reception of an underground station was what made you understand what underground really was. It was like I was down with some shit nobody else knew about. None of my so-called b-boy homeboys were fuckin' with these shows. I don't know if it was because of the schedules—the DNA & Hank Love and Awesome Two shows were on at way past midnight on Saturdays and Lyvio G & P-Fine was on Tuesdays at 9 PM—or if it was just that I was really a strung-out dope fiend. Back then, the only other ways you heard Hip Hop were either from a cassette on somebody's boombox or at a block party, period.

As far as videos, there were short-lived shows like *New York Hot Tracks* and *Graffiti Rock* (which only aired one episode) on the weekends. Fuck it, at least we still had *Soul Train*. I wouldn't miss Rosie Perez's big boobs for nothing on a Saturday morning.

But Ralph McDaniels' *Video Music Box* became the don of the shit from the first day it came on. Not only was he from the same New York streets Hip Hop was born on and a fan himself, but also, his show was on six days a week. He picked his time slot wisely. Actually, dude was brilliant; he had *Video Music Box* on right after school so that all the kids that were falling into the same addiction as me could get their fix as soon as they got home. Whereas you usually walked into your apartment, got a snack from the kitchen, and turned on the cable box to catch Woody Woodpecker, G.I. Joe and Inspector Gadget, now you didn't fuck with the cable box at all; you had to turn the TV to UHF, use the extra dial with the small numbers on it to turn to channel 31, mess with the antenna a little bit, and there it was, you were back in another dimension of the underground, but with images and in broad daylight.

You could also catch it at noon on Saturdays. There wasn't any *Yo! MTV Raps* or *Rap City* until years later.

Any VCR owned by me or my mother over the next twenty years basically became a video boombox. I had no less than six hours of music videos on each tape. Classic movies like *See No Evil, Hear No Evil, Speed,* and *Mantis vs. Falcon Claws* got recorded over with the quickness. Shit, even *Belly* with Nas and DMX and my niece's copy of *Home Alone* ain't get no mercy.

Nearly all the Jewish and Greek families had moved out of my building by then. My friend Toboland was also gone. My boy C-lo's family left to the Bronx early that year, Ant's family did the same not long after. As a matter of fact, it soon seemed like most of the Puerto Ricans, Cubans, and everything else there was in the hood were relocating to the Bronx and out of New York City altogether, and the only people moving in were Dominicans.

Around that time was when my little crew became aware that apartment 53 in our building was a whorehouse. Every Monday a different trio of women came to work there; they were mostly South Americans. If you were outside, you could tell who the hookers were because seven days a week they arrived at eleven in the morning and left at nine at night; those were the hours of operation at that whorehouse. All you had to look for was the unfamiliar faces going in and out of 600 at those times. While inside the whorehouse they wore lingerie, in the streets they were unassuming women, dressed like most of your friends' mothers; you wouldn't break your neck to get a second look at them. They charged fifteen dollars for fifteen minutes of pleasure.

This is how it worked: You would go into the living room to check out the merchandise. There might have been two ugly bitches there. So, you might have had to sit down and chill for a few minutes 'cause you wanted to see if the third hoe looked any good; she was somewhere in the apartment doing her thing with another client. When she finally came back into the living room, you either left or pointed out which one of them you wanted, the pimp gave you a playing card from a full deck—your ticket—and you followed the hoe you chose into one of the three bedrooms.

The whores would first clean your dick with baby wipes or a paper towel and alcohol, and then put the condom on you before getting busy. You just had to make sure you didn't ask them to ride you or if you could hit it from the back 'cause those bitches wouldn't do it; those dead fucks only made their money on their backs, literally. Ask for another position and they reacted as if you were asking them to do some acrobatic shit.

"*Ay, no, yo no voy a hacer eso. Eso es mucho trabajo*" ("Oh, hell no, I'm not going to do that. That's too much work"), they'd screw-face.

I was about seventeen the first time I went in there. But it was just to hang out afterhours. The pimp on duty, Nelson, invited my little crew of guys and girls known as the Large Criminals to go upstairs and chill out; wasn't nobody fuckin' or nothin'.

197

Within three months at One-forty-three, things were getting crazier for me over there; I was cutting classes and getting thrown out of them for doing stupid shit and getting into fights.

Stupid shit:

1. In this one class, we had to sit in alphabetical order. So, since my last name started with an A, I was at that first table. Our teacher Mrs. Smith was a woman that looked like she was straight out of the 1800's with deep cracks in her face that you would call wrinkles, and salt and pepper hair that resembled the bristles of a witch's broom, and whose talk was more like a whining scream and scream was a screeching cry. Whenever she got mad at me, she'd send me to sit all the way in the back of the classroom as if that was going to keep me from fucking around. Mrs. Smith had no idea that I liked sitting in the back, being close to the windows; looking outside took my mind out of One-forty-three.

On one of those days that I had been "punished", while she was writing on the blackboard and had her back to me, I put my chair on top of my desk and casually sat up there taking notes.

She turned around and jumped back at the sight of me. "Gustavo, what are you doing up there?!"

"Sorry, Mrs. Smith, I couldn't see what you were writing."

"Get down from there right now!" she screamed, her voice equal to a thousand nails scratching the blackboard behind her.

2. A couple of us would throw chairs out the third-floor classroom windows so that friends with names like Kid Shock and Midnite could

hang out on the corner comfortably after having escaped out the back door of the school earlier.

The long pole that was used to open and close windows got tossed out too. Luckily, the desks ain't fit through the windows.

3. My class once set up a playful rumble with another class in the basement. We tore their asses up, but my boy Dag did more than half the work. Dag was doing that UFC shit before it even existed. I remember he dove into that other class first, turning round and round like a mini tornado while letting off spinning backfists and elbows into kids' heads and faces. The next day, two other classes challenged us, and they got fucked up too.

I was in class 7K1 or 7W1, I don't remember too well. But it was said that if your class number ended with the number one, it meant it was the smartest in that grade (except for the classes that ended in SP and EP, those were the nerdy motherfuckers). So, the kids in my class weren't stupid, they were just knuckleheads. We never thought our misbehaving was a big deal, but we were all caught off-guard when almost half the class got left back.

When my father's businesses in Miami and California failed, that bastard had the nerve to move into his in-laws' home in our same building. At first, he used to try to sneak in and out without being seen. But after a while he got comfortable and occasionally hung out in the confines of his double-parked car up front. That disrespect of him living with another woman in the same building as us didn't hit me until I was an adult; he totally disregarded my family as if it wasn't once *his* family like if it was nothing; a man of better principles would have taken that L and gone to a shelter. But at thirteen years old, I was just excited to have him close by.

Every few weeks, I'd sneak up to apartment 24 in the early evenings to spend some time with *Papi*, nervously knocking on the door while looking both ways, hoping none of my neighbors saw me going inside; my mother would have flipped if she had known. It was a gamble going into that apartment 'cause it was right between the homes of my homies Boogie and Washington, and *their* mothers knew *my* mother; coming in and out was a stealth mission, just like at the whorehouse, which was three floors directly above Boogie's crib.

My father and his wife were living in a cramped room. It was stacked with boxes of whatever merchandise he still had left over to sell. A lot had changed for him since back when we had a full house as a warehouse in Puerto Rico.

While there, he never really spoke to me much; they'd give me milk and cookies like if I was a little fuckin' kid; *I was thirteen*. It was a waste of time sitting there with him while his undivided attention was on the Spanish soap operas playing on the TV. I used to feel uneasy and wonder what I was doing there. Every time I was ready to leave, he would persuade me into staying a little longer. I didn't know how to say no to my father. When I agreed to stay, in anticipation that he might finally make some conversation with me, it never happened. I just sat there going brain-dead from watching another hour or two of those boring-as-fuck, mind-numbing shows. Until one night I felt so restless that I couldn't take another second of it. Pops begged me to stay but I got up and headed for the door without hesitation.

"Nah, I'm out."

"Por favor, quédate un ratito mas." ("Please stay a little while longer.")

"I'll come see you tomorrow." I lied as I strolled out the door and straight down the stairs, moving through the building lobby quickly as if I was running late for a rendezvous with my beloved streets. I felt like I was having way more fun and learning way more shit out there anyway. Pops ain't have shit to offer me besides cookies and milk and a healthy dose of claustrophobia in him and his wife's bedroom-slash-storage room.

But yeah, as crazy as it sounds, the monotony of those soap operas full of plastic people was what actually helped build up the courage in me to finally rebel against my father for the first time in my life. I was outta there and never went back.

Children's Story

1982. The 6th Floor.

I'm sitting on the steps next to the elevator. Bighead Benny and Mikey are standing right in front of me. We're having a conversation about the differences in our schools. Me and Mikey are in PS 132, and Benny is in Saint Elizabeth's.

"That shit is wack, though, Benny. Your parents have to pay for you to go there and you have to wear a uniform."

"Yeah, my parents pay, but so what? I bet I'll get a better education than you guys. And a uniform looks better than the way a lot of other kids go to school. Trust me, I've seen some of these kids dressing like little bums on their way to PS One-thirty-two!"

"Nah, hell no!" Mikey laughs.

"Nah, Benny." I was quietly listening to the debate until then.

"If you ask me, that shit is a waste of time; school is school. They just be trying to have y'all looking fancy with those funky-ass uniforms!" Mikey continues. "That shit is corny."

"No, it's not."

"Yes, it is."

"No, it's not!" Bighead Benny's undiagnosed gayness shows up just a little bit right at that moment. "Wearing a uniform is a display of organization! Like the army! We follow rules!"

"Y'all ain't no soldiers! Catholic school niggas are soft!"

"We're organized! I bet there's a whole bunch of little bums acting all wild in One-thirty-two! Do you know that most of you that go to public schools will end up on drugs or in jail?"

"Say what?" I get back in the conversation with a cringe.

"Get the fuck outta here with that bullshit, Bighead!"

"I'm telling you, it's true!"

"Nah, Benny, you buggin'.", I say, "There's no way of telling which one of us are gonna fuck up in life. That's bullshit, man."

"You guys don't have to believe me. I know it's true."

"How do you know it's true? Who told you that?"

"Nobody told me. I just know it."

"Yeah, I don't believe you. Somebody put that in your head."

"Fuck that, Benny! Kids that go to catholic school are not better than kids that go to public school! They probably worse!"

"Word, Benny, that's a crazy way to look at the world."

"For real! You saying that me and Gus and Erin and Jay are gonna be dope fiends while you some rich lawyer living the good life in a penthouse and shit! You not better than us, Benny!"

"I'm not saying that, Mikey!"

"That's exactly what'chu saying!"

"You can't front, Benny, that *is* what you're saying."

"We gonna see what happens in the future, Bighead.", Mikey disappointedly says as he turns down his voice, visibly insulted by his best friend, his face looking like his heart is crushed even worse from Bighead Benny's words than the racism he's endured all along from most of the kids in the building. "You gonna fuck around and be the one strung-out out here in these streets."

"I'm not trying to argue with you, Mikey. All I know is that it's a fact: if you go to public schools and not catholic schools, most of you will wind up either drug addicts or in jail."

"We'll see."

Furious Five on the train ride,

I keep my eyes on the boombox

Absorbing the rhymes,

gotta get off in two stops

Melle Mel, Spoonie Gee & LL

made me wanna rhyme

DJ Tito was killing it

at the pool in the summertime

I wanted those twelve-hundreds,

got me some Panasonics

My family's so broke,

might as well have no pockets

I'm a preteen,

all I ever seen is a dope & a weed fiend

It's bugged,

Hip Hop is the number one drug on the street scene

But that's changin'

coke is on the verge of an invasion

New guns on the street are makin'

criminals more brazen

Uzis & tecs

when used loosely they wet

multiple bystanders,

the area is filled with mourning, despair, & anger

Adidas, Fat laces, windbreakers, & cardboard

We just little kids

but life in The Heights

still hardcore

Cheo chasing us with his gun

like it's a murder-for-hire

Meanwhile

I'm having thoughts of

setting the other drunk on fire

Not even old enough to drink beers

& already my peers

predictin', I'll be livin' on prison tiers

For committing genocide & homicide on the streets

I wish I could just go back to the train ride & the beats

That second joint will be lit sooner than you think.

Acknowledgements

I want to thank God for giving me this journey, being there when I needed him most to survive it and keeping me here long enough to tell my story. To my mother, my number one supporter and the greatest love I ever knew. I can see you somewhere reading this and saying, "You did it, baby!" To my sisters Cookie, Tish, and Aggie for helping me learn how to read and write, giving me the tools to express myself and everything else in your arsenal that turned me into a productive human being. To my wife Angie, thank you for your patience, buying me my Mac to write on, and getting me the hell off the streets finally. You and the girls were the strongest piece to changing my life. To my daughters Destiny, Angelina, and Jayda for always believing in me and being the greatest advisors I could ever have on this project. To my father, because without you as an example, whether good or bad, I couldn't have been all that I am to my own children. I appreciate your uncanny love for the hustle and aspire to surpass it with my own. All in all, you are a great father with many flaws. But so many of us are. To my homeboy Juni, whose name I used as my pseudonym. While rappers have used everything from the names of movie characters, Italian mobsters, and big-time drug dealers and stick up kids they never met as their aliases, I chose to use the name of an actual friend and pay homage to you. The streets took you early and you never even made it to the 90's, so I decided to give your name the shine you never had a chance to give it on your own. Tell Bruce Lee I said what's up and that I waited for him longer than you did. I'll see you when I get there. To all the friends, enemies, and all others that crossed paths with me, you taught me lessons and helped shape and mold me into the person I've become, no matter if we knew each other all of our lives, or it was just through a fraction-of-a-second glance that took place anywhere from a crowded uptown bodega to the gritty streets of the old Hell's Kitchen to the beautiful sands of Honolulu.

I Appreciate You All.

A special thank you to all the MC's whose lyrics influenced me and which I used in this book in order to educate the readers. I'm forever indebted to you for your inspiration and guidance.

Sadat X on A Tribe Called Quest – Award Tour (1993)

Sugarhill Gang – Rapper's Delight (1979)

Spoonie Gee – Spoonin' Rap (1979)

Biz Markie Ft. TJ Swan – Nobody Beats the Biz (1987)

Public Enemy – Welcome to The Terrordome (1990)

Just-Ice – That Girl is A Slut (1986)

Kool Moe Dee – Go See the Doctor (1986)

Kool G Rap & DJ Polo – Rikers Island (1987)

T La Rock & Jazzy Jay – It's Yours (1984)

Ultramagnetic MC's - Ego Tripping (1986)

Peace

Outside Apartment 38: Broken Language Vol. 1 is a work of nonfiction. Some names and identifying details have been changed.

Copyright © 2019 by Juni

Published in the United States of America by 80s Dopehouse Publishing.

ISBN 978-0-578-43923-5 (eBook)
ISBN 978-0-578-43942-6 (print)

Made in the USA
Middletown, DE
19 February 2019